The
ULTIMATE
WOOD
BLOCK
BOOK

Building Castles, Bridges & Other Engineering Marvels

■ ■ ■ ■ ■

Sam Bingham

D1567283

Sterling Publishing Co., Inc. New York

To my father and two grandfathers
whose playful delight in human ingenuity
assured them eternal youth.

Edited by Carol Palmer

Bingham, Sam.
    The ultimate wood block book : building castles, bridges &
other engineering marvels / Sam Bingham.
        p. cm.
    Includes index.
    ISBN 0-8069-6662-9 (pbk.)
    1. Wooden toy making. 2. Blocks (Toys) I. Title.
TT174.5.W6B554 1988   88-21700
745.592—dc19   CIP

Copyright © 1988 by Sam Bingham
Published by Sterling Publishing Co., Inc.
387 Park Avenue South, New York, N.Y. 10016
Distributed in Canada by Oak Tree Press Ltd.
% Canadian Manda Group, P.O. Box 920, Station U
Toronto, Ontario, Canada M8Z 5P9
Distributed in Great Britain and Europe by Cassell PLC
Artillery House, Artillery Row, London SW1P 1RT, England
Distributed in Australia by Capricorn Ltd.
P.O. Box 665, Lane Cove, NSW 2066
Manufactured in the United States of America

Sterling ISBN 0-8069-6662-9 Paper

▪ Contents ▪

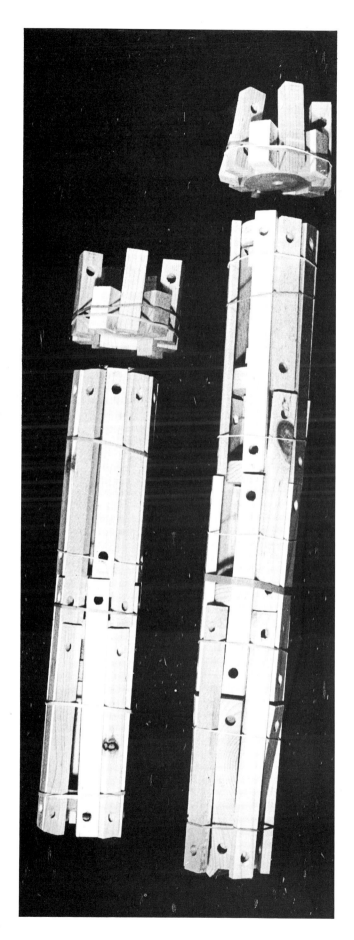

▪ Introduction ▪
Why Make a Set
of Blocks?

Many parents think nothing of spending hundreds of dollars for a swing set, sand box, bicycle, or gaudy electronic ray guns in order to keep Junior occupied in a reasonably constructive way without intruding on the grown-up world. However, such toys wear out, children grow out of them rapidly, and they work best outdoors. Commercially made toy construction sets are wonderful toys, and have educational value as well—but to buy enough to occupy several kids at once costs a fortune, and most of the pieces work on only one building principle.

On the other hand, for less than half the cost of a new bicycle, you can make enough blocks to entertain a whole kindergarten day after day. They will last literally for generations. They are safe for the smallest baby, and every subsequent age will find them a challenge.

This book describes the making of a Block Set, and a Block Box to keep the pieces in, and 40 projects of varying sophistication that you can build from the blocks. These projects not only show the range of possibilities that can be achieved with this set, but also enable the serious block builder to experience in a very genuine way some of the world's great moments of architecture and engineering. Some of the projects in this book represent famous examples in the history of architecture and engineering. As they illustrate most of the principles used in real structures, a committed block builder will learn quite sophisticated engineering skills. Other projects are

just for fun, like the marble slide, rubber-band cars, or catapult.

Using rubber bands and dowels to hold blocks together is a new idea and all of the projects show tricks for doing it. Even if you don't try to build the complicated projects like Harlech Castle and Chartres Cathedral, they still contain many ideas useful when building walls, towers of different kinds, and roofs.

Making the basic Block Set demands only the most rudimentary operations in all of carpentry: sawing and drilling. You only need two power tools: a table saw, and a drill press; and the latter can be any kind of bench-top affair that will drill a straight hole. Only a weekend or two, seven 6-foot pine planks, lots of dowelling, and a little plywood is needed to make the set.

The old-style kindergarten blocks have some limitations. They take up an enormous

amount of space, weigh a lot, and one can only build by stacking them. The design shown here, however, overcomes all of those problems. By making the blocks half the thickness of the common style, one can in fact fit four times the number into the same space. The addition of holes and dowels makes them even more versatile. Because rubber bands are light and small, common and infinitely available, we use them to replace the specially made fittings that render many construction sets useless when they disappear into the sofa cushions. Building arches with these blocks also requires masking tape, but again, a pittance will buy enough at any supermarket to last nearly forever. Even the great trial of picking up such toys goes better with blocks that stack in a satisfying way and fit neatly in the Block Box.

▪ Introduction 2 ▪
Four Generations
of Building-Block
Engineers

One evening, I went with Dad to visit *his* father, "Pops." Pops read a book about ancient Rome. Dad doodled with a pocket slide rule and made notes about projects he had in mind. I dumped out an old family set of blocks and began to build a small house for myself, then a road, and at the end of the road I meant to build a house for a magic friend. But the road ran into a row of magazines. I started to bulldoze them aside with blocks.

Dad's eyes did not leave the slide rule, but his voice said, "You can't do that. That's a river. You'll have to build a bridge."

I stood blocks on the magazines and laid my bridge across. Dad shifted on the couch and his foot accidentally touched the magazines, and my blocks came down like dominoes.

"Fast river and poor footings," said Dad. "I guess you'll have to cross it in a single span. Bridge it from side-to-side with nothing in the middle to hold it up."

I couldn't. The longest block wouldn't nearly reach. I looked at Dad. Dad put the slide rule back in its leather case. "I suppose," he said in a very serious voice, "I suppose it's time you learned about cantilevers."

"Cantilevers?"

"Yes," said Dad bending towards me from the couch. "That's when you build out over the water without holding up your blocks from the other side or from underneath. Like this," he said, stretching out one arm and

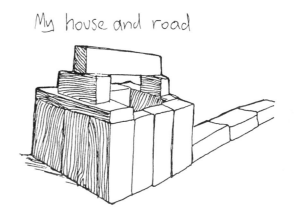

My house and road

My first bridge

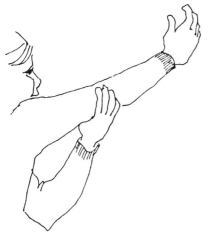

A cantilevered arm

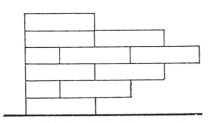

Corbels - blocks held out by the weight of other blocks.

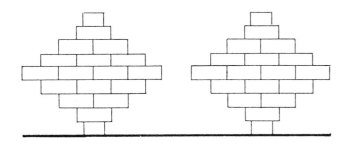

resting the elbow on the other hand. You don't have rivets and steel like modern bridge builders," he added, "so we'll have to make a corbelled cantilever. We'll use the weight of two blocks to hold one block farther out."

By the time Dad said "we" instead of "you," he already had blocks in both hands. We built two cantilever bridge towers, but the "river" was too wide and they did not meet. We tried adding another course of blocks, but wrecked the towers.

Pops's book lay closed beside him on the couch. Now a volume of his old encyclopedia lay across his knees, opened to the article on bridges. "I seem to remember that you and I learned something from the Quebec Bridge in Canada," he said to Dad. "The first tower they built collapsed and killed 75 men. They had to start all over. As I recall, they built two towers like yours, then put a small bridge between them. They built that central span ashore, then floated it out on barges and hoisted it into place."

"That's right," said Dad, showing me the pictures Pops had found. "Didn't they accidentally drop the first span into the harbor and have to build a second?"

"Indeed," said Pops. "So did we!" But by then Dad had turned into a steam tugboat that said "chichichichichi" as it hauled our central span to mid-channel. Then we both became winches at the ends of our cantilevers, and hauled the span into position.

For a long time, Pops and Dad and I sat together on the floor looking at the bridge.

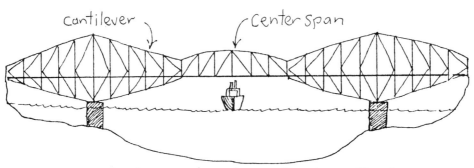

cantilever   center span

The steel construction Quebec Bridge

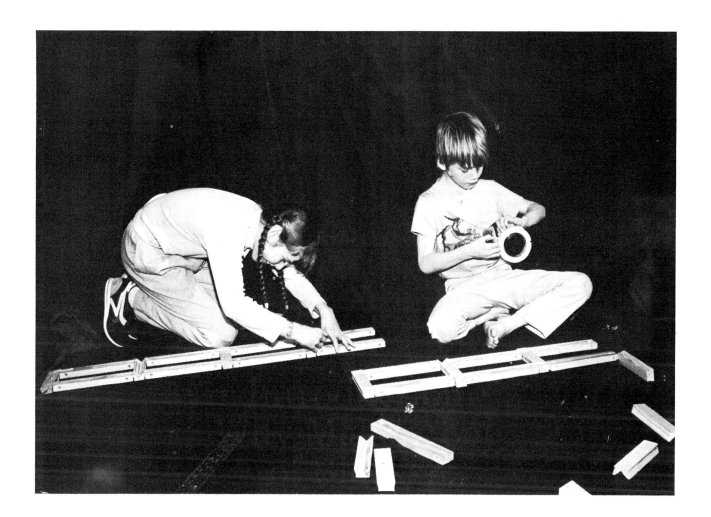

"It's too bad we can't build like the ancient Romans," Pops said at last. "They would have arched that stream, but we can't do that with wooden blocks."

"No," said Dad, "we can't build real cantilevers or trusses either. You have to have an erector set for that, but there's something nice about real wooden blocks."

"A corbelled cantilever isn't bad," I said.

We built so many things, Dad and Pops and I—Greek temples (Pops loved Greece as much as Rome), huge suspension bridges that the rest of the family ducked beneath to enter or leave the room, a travelling crane that lifted blocks to the tops of skyscrapers, and the Cretan maze of Minos with a live Minotaur in the middle.

Somewhat later, I made a pine box and filled it with blocks for my own son and daughter, Kevin and Robin (at least I said it was for them). Like all Block Boxes, it has a certain magic in it. You can put one thing in it today, and take out something different tomorrow.

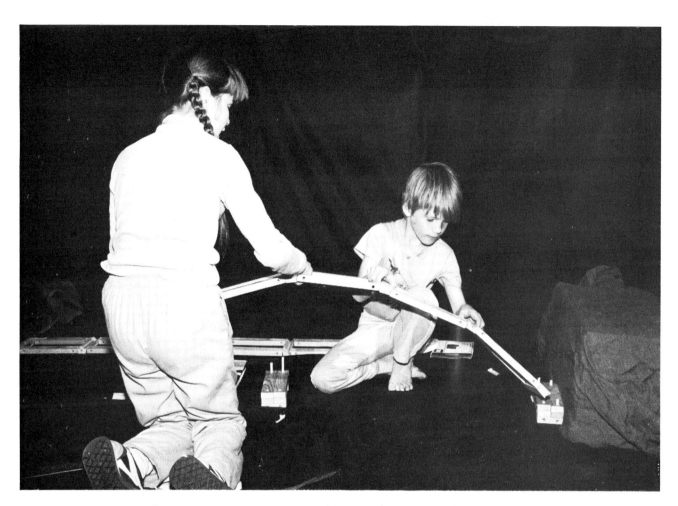

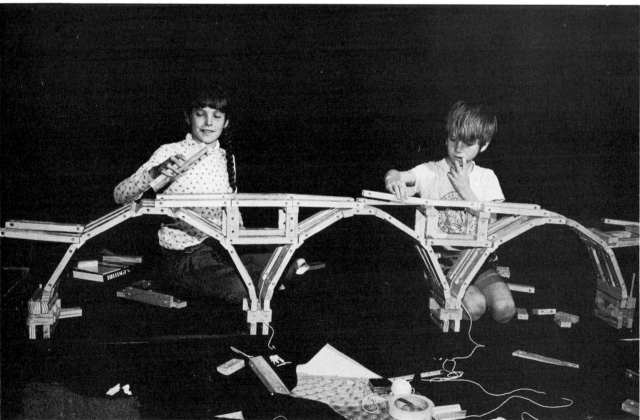

· 1 ·
Making the Block Set

Making the Blocks

Given a running start and the material and jigs on hand, I have made a whole set of blocks in a single long day. From scratch, I'd say the uninitiated might do it in two weekends. The blocks for all the projects in this book can be rendered from the following materials.

Materials

> 40 running feet of 1″ × 12″ pine
> 6 feet of 2″ × 8″ pine (⁶⁄₄″ × 6″ is better if available), if possible without rounded edges.
> 10 pieces of 3-foot long ⁵⁄₁₆″-diameter dowel
> 1¹¹⁄₃₂″ drill bit for the drill press
> 1 hollow ground planer blade for the table saw (don't confuse it with a combination blade which looks nearly the same to the naked eye)
> 1 2½″ hole saw for making wheels

(METRIC NOTE: Fortunately, in most metric countries a standard board is 19 mm, which is only about .05 mm larger than ¾″. A common 38-mm timber is also virtually the same as the North American 2″ or ⁶⁄₄″ equivalent. The conversion to a 19-mm block unit is a simple matter. Holes and dowels are also encountered in the Block Set's construction. In North America an ¹¹⁄₃₂″ hole for a ⁵⁄₁₆″ dowel works perfectly. In metric, 8-mm dowels in 9-mm holes will work, though they will be a bit looser than the American combination allows. An 8.5-mm hole will be a little tighter.)

Someday I intend to make the Block Set from maple, cherry, dogwood, or even walnut in order to produce a truly classy heirloom. Nevertheless, humble pine has definite advantages:

- It's cheap and easy to get.
- It works easily and fast.
- Lifting a set of pine blocks won't break your back.

- Pine blocks make less noise when kids let their buildings crash.
- The edges soon become rounded without sanding, and thus more comfortable to play with.

I have used white pine, ponderosa pine, and southern yellow pine. The first two are very similar. The southern pine is harder, heavier, and in many respects more satisfying, but the heavy grain sometimes deflects the drill in an annoying way. Naturally, any wood that tends to splinter, such as cedar or redwood, would not serve.

CHOOSING YOUR MATERIAL

The struggle for precision begins in the lumberyard. Theoretically, you could buy the cheapest junk on the lot because, except for the box itself, you need nothing longer than 9″. However, six 6-footers of a good grade will not break you and will save hours of time. The best sawyer in the world can't rip a straight cut through a board that would rather be a pretzel, and the planer blade will bind at the slightest excuse.

- Avoid large red knots. They make truly agonizing work out of ripping and drilling, and often indicate that the board is waiting to pinch or twist the minute the blade cuts into it. Black knots may ruin a block or two, but seldom bind the saw.
- Beware of boards that contain the pith from the center of the log. They, more than others, may have hidden stresses.
- Get absolutely flat, absolutely straight boards. You can never make truly vertical cuts in a board that cups even slightly. You can accept some wane on the edges and even some bad knots, but no warps of any kind.
- Check the thickness of every board in several places. The liberal interpretations of the standard ¾″ plank that you can find in a lumberyard might astound you. Usually, boards from the same stack resemble each other. Be careful about taking one old board from a previous project and buying the others. Take a sample and hold it against

the boards in the yard. Your fingers will feel small differences in thickness better than your ruler can measure them. Try to get an exact ¾″, but at least get all of your boards the same.

Lumber in hand, go home and start ripping it at once. A day behind the workbench with one end in the sun, a week on sawhorses in the shed, or time spent lying on the floor with one side exposed to dry air can twist the frail soul of a 1″ × 12″ beyond redemption. It will keep much better when ripped into narrow strips.

ACCURACY
Cutting and drilling some 600 small pieces that must relate to each other in a reasonably precise way involves aspects of mass production which don't bedevil the average shop project. Before you're done with the Block Set, you will have a profound admiration for those wizards of industry who manage to combine quality and productivity in the manufacture of cars, cameras, and electronic gimmicks.

Wood, especially soft pine, is not a precise medium compared to plastic or steel, and ordinary hand-fed shop tools often lack the over-built rigidity of their industrial counterparts. You cannot, therefore, simply set the rip fence (saw) and the drilling jig (drill) and forget about them. You must sample and check your production frequently.

The checking itself has pitfalls, because you must spot deviations too small to see or even measure easily. A small measurement like one 32nd of an inch means nothing to an individual block, but it adds up to a full quarter-inch in a stack of eight blocks. On the other hand, since a few nonstandard blocks in a stack seldom make much difference, you will come out all right if the range of imperfections isn't too wide and averages out to zero.

Having reduced a good many feet of lumber to worthless small bits by failing to recheck accuracy, I have developed some simple tests to catch creeping imprecision, and have described them below. As you will rapidly discover, precision and productivity are about the only difficulties presented by this project.

RIPPING
Of the 40 feet of 1″ × 12″, 32 feet should make all the blocks with room to spare. The extra serves for box cleats, wheels, drilling jigs and insurance. You will rip strips of three different widths in the following proportions. (Save the scraps for emergencies.)

- From 30 feet of the 1″ × 12″ pine you will make 210 feet of strips ¾″ × 1½″.
- From 3½ feet of the 1″ × 12″ pine you will make 45½ feet of strips ¾″ × ¾″.
- From 3½ feet of the 1″ × 12″ pine you will make 80½ feet of strips ⅜″ × ¾″.

At this point throw away your ruler; you will not use it again. Since the blocks will only be measured against each other, you should only use blocks to measure blocks.

BLOCK UNITS AND BLOCK NAMES
The Block Set, like most construction toys, is designed around a basic unit. In order to avoid having to have a measuring stick at hand at all times, the instructions for the block projects in this book will refer to blocks in terms of the length in block units. One block unit is the thickness of the board from which all are cut, in this case ¾″, which for obscure reasons is the standard thickness of what is sold as a 1″ board in North America.

Going by cross section (what you see when looking at the blocks end-on), the blocks fall into three classes—wide, square, and thin, according to the three kinds of strips from which they are cut. Lengths range from 2 to 12 block units. For brevity we will talk from now on about A, B, and C blocks instead of wide, square, or thin blocks, with the length in block units as the second part of the name. The chart on page 16 shows the quantity and sizes of each block type.

ADJUSTING THE RIP FENCE
The majority of the blocks are twice as wide as thick. Illus. 1.1 shows the rip fence adjusted to the thickness of two blocks. The chances of getting it right the first time are small. Cut and check on pieces of scrap until you are sure you have it perfect.

Illus. 1.1   The rip fence adjusted to the thickness of two blocks

Illus. 1.2   Checking four blocks against two for accuracy

Illus. 1.2 shows the process of checking four blocks against two. That will double the effect of any error and make it easier to spot. Even then, try the six blocks in different combinations to make sure you don't have a freak that happens to cancel out a real mistake.

Follow the same procedure when ripping the narrower widths. Cutting four ⅜" strips that stack to exactly the width of your 1½" strip is no mean feat. However, in the context of the way the narrow blocks are usually used in structures, absolute perfection is seldom required.

RIPPING GUIDE

Illus. 1.3 shows a ripping guide made from a scrap of 1" × 8". When used as in Illus. 1.4 it will hold a board against the rip fence better than anyone working along with a longish board can by hand. A block clamped to the fence itself keeps the board from riding up over the blade.

Even with the guide, however, boards over 6 feet get pretty unwieldy and, again, the slightest wiggle of either end of the plank as it passes the saw will cause a deviation of the cut which can also distort the next pass as well. If you buy your lumber in 8 to 12 foot lengths, cut it down before ripping.

CUTTING OFF

The chart shows the dimensions and quantities of blocks and accessories that make up the basic Block Set. A radial arm saw is the ideal tool for reducing the ripped strips into

Illus. 1.3   Ripping guide made from scrap

Illus. 1.4   The ripping guide in use

THE BASIC BLOCK SET

Block Name	Quantity	Dimensions In Inches	Dimensions In Block Units	
Wide				
A12	32	¾″ × 1½″ × 9″	1 × 2 × 12	
A10	22	¾″ × 1½″ × 7½″	1 × 2 × 10	Drill two
A8	100	¾″ × 1½″ × 6″	1 × 2 × 8	perpendicular
A4	156	¾″ × 1½″ × 3″	1 × 2 × 4	holes in each end
A2	20	¾″ × 1½″ × 1½″	1 × 2 × 2	
Square				
B12	20	¾″ × ¾″ × 9″	1 × 1 × 12	
B8	24	¾″ × ¾″ × 6″	1 × 1 × 8	Drill one hole in
B4	26	¾″ × ¾″ × 3″	1 × 1 × 4	each end
B2	20	¾″ × ¾″ × 1½″	1 × 1 × 2	
Thin				
C12	40	⅜″ × ¾″ × 9″	½ × 1 × 12	
C10	40	⅜″ × ¾″ × 7½″	½ × 1 × 10	Drill one hole in
C8	32	⅜″ × ¾″ × 6″	½ × 1 × 8	each end
Arch Blocks (see Illus. 1.8 for dimensions)				
D8	20	6″ long	8 block units long	
D4	20	3″ long	4 block units long	
D2	32	1½″ long	2 block units long	
Notched Arch Blocks (see Illus. 1.9 and 1.10 for dimensions)				
E8	10	6″ long	8 block units long	
E4	10	3″ long	4 block units long	
E2	16	1½″ long	2 block units long	

Dowels

Cut a starter set from ten 3-foot lengths of ⁵⁄₁₆″-diameter dowel:

	15	4¼″ long
	20	5⅝″ long
	20	7″ long

Ramps

Two or more A8 blocks sliced according to Illus. 1.19.

Wheels

8 or more cut with a 2½″ hole saw from scrap lumber 1 block unit thick

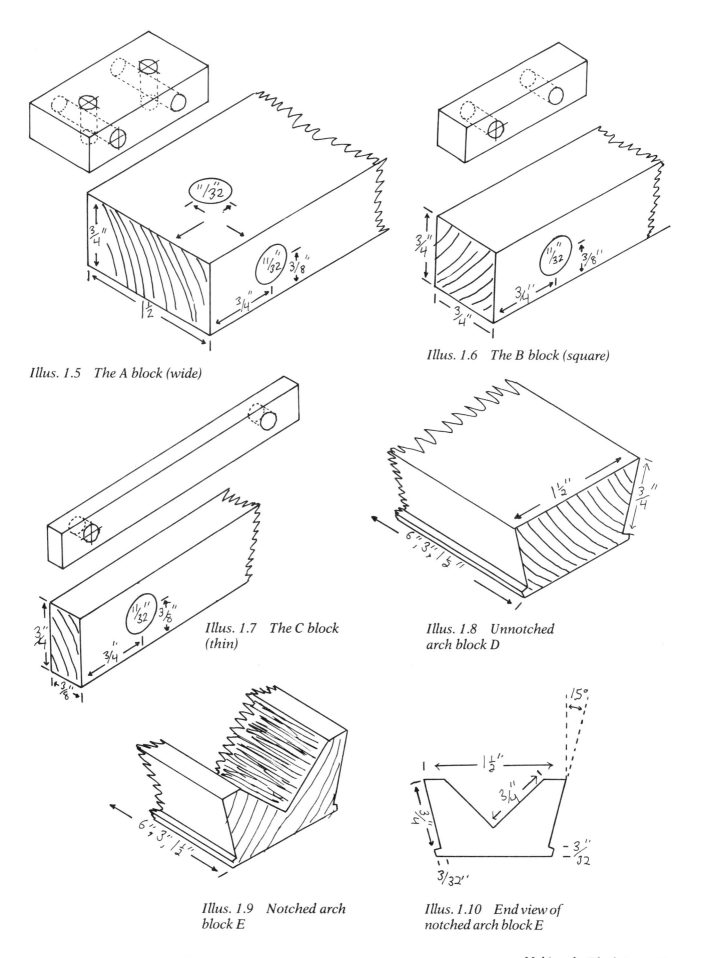

Illus. 1.5   The A block (wide)

Illus. 1.6   The B block (square)

Illus. 1.7   The C block (thin)

Illus. 1.8   Unnotched arch block D

Illus. 1.9   Notched arch block E

Illus. 1.10   End view of notched arch block E

blocks, but a table saw will serve. Illus. 1.11 shows a method of pushing blocks past a table saw blade with a back-up block that rises above the height of the saw. Without it, blocks can turn and bind between the blade and the rip fence. That wrecks the blocks, may wreck the saw, and occasionally will fire a piece of wood into the pit of your stomach.

Once again, use the blocks themselves to set up the rip fence as in Illus. 1.12, and check the result (Illus. 1.13). Use more than one selection of blocks to make this test. Check the same distance using the *width* of your strips, and recheck from time to time. Banging strips against the rip fence at the beginning of the cut can move it ever so slightly, and every block after that is junk. Cut the longest blocks first; then work down to the smallest.

Don't try to select strips that have no knots or bad spots at the cut-off points. Simply toss any blocks that turn out badly into a scrap pile and use them when cutting the next-smaller size. The waste will be minimal, and the production line attitude will save a great deal of time.

DRILLING

Drilling the hundreds of holes required in a full set of these blocks is as great a task as cutting the blocks themselves. A light bench drill press and one sharp $^{11}/_{32}$" bit will do the job, but again, precision is a major challenge.

If at all possible, obtain a professional cabinetmaker's bit, called a "brad point." It has a central spike and sharp skirts like the wood bits that go in a hand brace. It will center itself without skating around and the skirts score the outline of the hole, leaving no splinters or tear-out. Why hardware dealers seldom carry such bits is a mystery, as they eliminate one of the most irritating frustrations of home carpentry. They cost about six dollars from an industrial tool supplier or specialty house. Any local cabinet shop should be able to give you a good local source, if not lend you one.

Illus. 1.14 shows a drilling jig. Experience has shown that the jig really only needs stops on one side and one end. The single upright

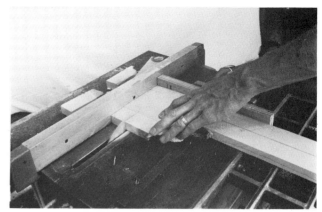

Illus. 1.11   A method for feeding blocks through the rip fence

Illus. 1.12   Use the blocks to set the rip fence.

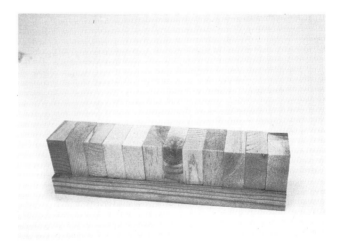

Illus. 1.13   Check blocks against each other for accuracy.

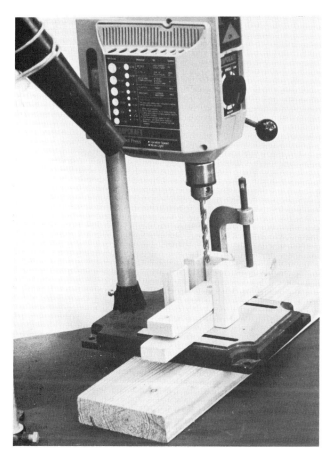

Illus. 1.14   The drilling jig

at the jig (top left corner). That cured the problem. Later, however, I discovered that I could clamp the end piece so as to leave a healthy gap between it and the side, and I could puff away the shavings with my own lungs.

All blocks 1½″ wide (A blocks) get drilled in two directions at each end, the narrower blocks (B and C blocks) only in one direction (see Illus. 1.5, 1.6, and 1.7). All holes center one block-width back from the end. When adjusting the jig, use a block to measure and scribe this point on another block. After the holes are drilled, use a machinist's square as in Illus. 1.15 to check accuracy. The distance to the edge of the hole should be the same from both sides and the end.

Even small irregularities will show up if you stack the blocks on a pair of dowels as in Illus. 1.16.

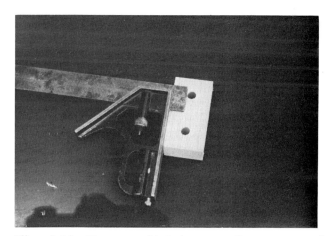

Illus. 1.15   Use a machinist's square for accuracy of dowel holes.

block on the right of the one in the photo is not necessary.

In this case, the base piece is bolted through the slots in the drill press stage to the board underneath. Before tightening the bolts all the way, you can center the jig by gentle taps on one side or the other.

The end of the jig, which sets how far from the end of the block the hole will fall, is a separate L-shaped piece. Illus. 1.14 shows the C-clamp which holds it in place by gripping the long end of the L.

The two-part jig has great advantages over a single-piece one simply bolted down. You can tap and tinker until the bit will come down in the center of the block; then adjust the L piece to get the hole the proper distance from the end without the risk of undoing your first setting.

Shavings in the corner of the jig were a great headache at first. Illus. 1.14 shows the blowing end of the shop vacuum aimed down

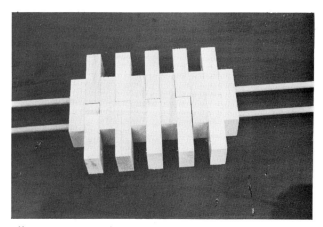

Illus. 1.16   Stack the blocks on dowels to check accuracy.

A big drill press can handle a stack of four or five easily when drilling the short dimension. Two at a time is a handful when drilling the long way.

ARCH BLOCKS

The arch blocks (see Illus. 1.8, 1.9, and 1.10) are cut from the 2″ × 8″ (or ⁶⁄₄″ × 6″) pine.

Rip it into 6 strips about 1³⁄₃₂″ thick. Extreme precision doesn't matter here, but 1⅛″ is a bit thick from the aesthetic standpoint, and 1¹⁄₁₆″ a bit thin from the structural standpoint.

The bevels (see Illus. 1.10) are 15°. To set the saw accurately, it is best to draw and cut this angle out of cardboard (Illus. 1.17). A good protractor will do the job. Test the 15° angle after facing the first strip on both sides by cutting off six short sample pieces. If you lay these out in an arch with five A2 blocks in the spaces between them, you should get a full semicircle, and the faces of the end blocks should line up perfectly against a straight edge.

You can cut the step in the edge of the arch block in one pass by bolting two blades into the saw as shown in Illus. 1.18. Typically, planer blades come in 5″ or 6½″ sizes, and any blade bigger than that can go on the outside of the cut.

Illus. 1.18 shows the two blades in action. The saw has been cranked up so that the planer blade leaves a face exactly as wide as the edge of a standard block. All strips are faced on both sides as seen in the photo.

One third of all the arch blocks also have a ¾″ notch cut in the broad side as noted in Illus. 1.9 and 1.10. To do this, adjust the planer blade alone to a 45° angle and pass the strip over the saw twice. It will take a bit of trial and error to get the rip fence and the depth of the cut exact.

Notch one third of your total footage of faced strips in this way, and you are ready to cut arch blocks to length in the same way as the other blocks. You will want 1½″, 3″, and 6″ lengths (2, 4, and 8 block unit lengths). Each arch length has four arch blocks and two notched arch blocks.

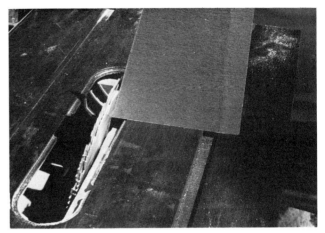
Illus. 1.17 Draw and cut the bevel angle out of cardboard to set the saw for the arch blocks.

Illus. 1.18 Cutting the sides of the arch blocks

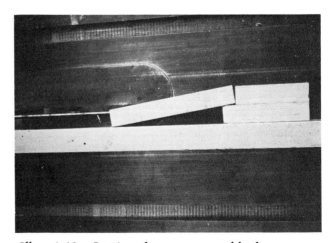
Illus. 1.19 Cutting slopes on ramp blocks

DOWELS

At various times during the life of the Block Set you will probably purchase more ⁵⁄₁₆″ dowels for building special projects and replacing those that wind up under the couch. However, ten 3-footers cut to the lengths indicated in the chart on page 16 will handle most projects. I can't justify these dimensions or quantities except to say that my own children, given a hacksaw and an unlimited supply of dowels over the years, have cut most of them to these lengths, and they cover most needs.

Some of the projects in this book require more dowels, or dowels in special lengths. You will not regret having another half-dozen 3-footers on hand to use when you need them. The Block Box has plenty of room. In a pinch, pencils will serve quite well as dowels.

RAMP BLOCKS

Kids love to drive trucks on and off the roads and bridges they make, but the square end of a block often hinders this. Four or five gentle slopes cut from A8 blocks solve the problem. Illus. 1.19 shows an easy way to feed these through the saw.

WHEELS

Wheels in any number (eight makes a good start) can be cut from scraps that are one block unit thick with a 2½″ hole saw in the drill press.

Most hole saws leave a ¼″ hole in the center, and this must be drilled out to ¹¹⁄₃₂″. When you do this, have a pair of big channel-lock pliers on hand to hold the wheel, or make a clamp out of scraps. The bit will seize the wheel and spin it viciously. If you try to secure it by hand, the ragged edge left by the saw will take revenge on your thumb. Use the clamp or the pliers, but let the wheel spin when it seizes. Then hold sandpaper against it until it seems smooth. Lastly, catch it with your pliers and pull it down off the spinning bit.

Illus. 1.20   The finished Block Box

Making the Block Box

A Block Set, complete with wheels, dowels, and rubber bands, adds up to many hundreds of small pieces which tend to accumulate under beds and beneath sofa cushions if not stored well. Thus, a good storage box is crucial.

Altogether, the blocks themselves occupy 2,227.5 cubic inches. The arches plus a roll of tape take up 472.5 cubic inches, and wheels, dowels, and rubber bands yet a bit more. All of it will go handily into a chest about the size of a small footlocker.

Originally, I made such a box by arranging the blocks in a neat stack, taking the measurements plus a little extra for slack, and adding a bit of depth so that I could toss dowels, wheels and other odd pieces on top of the lot. The arch blocks I kept separately in some old oatmeal boxes, as only the older children and more intelligent adults in the neighborhood used them.

I recommend this arrangement, however, only if you are making the Block Set as a gift for someone you don't expect to see again. Even pine blocks make such a box dangerously heavy for the weak of back, though putting it on casters mitigates this problem somewhat. Worse, however, is the fact that you can't build even the simplest item without dumping out the whole set, crash. Then, picking up is a chore.

The design here for a series of stacking trays solves both of those problems. One can get at a piece of any size without disturbing the rest, and though the total box is heavier, the individual trays are fairly light. The plans are for plywood construction, reinforced by pine strips. A good cabinetmaker could make something of the same dimensions far more elegantly and probably spend less time on it, but the plywood solution has the advantage of being a bit lighter to carry and more forgiving to the amateur carpenter.

The trays, numbered from the bottom up, are filled as follows:

- Tray 1 contains all the arch blocks, leaving space for a roll of masking tape laid flat.
- Tray 2 holds all 10- and 12-unit blocks (A's, B's, and C's), leaving space for four A4's in addition.
- Tray 3 holds all 8-unit blocks (A's, B's, and C's).
- In Tray 4 the large compartment holds the remaining 4- and 2-unit blocks exactly. Wheels, dowels, rubber bands, ramp blocks, etc., can go in the small compartment.

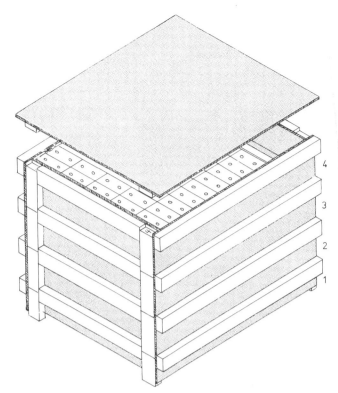

Illus. 1.21   Order of trays in the Block Box

Materials

    1 1" × 12" × 10-foot pine board with
          few or no knots
    1 4-foot × 8-foot sheet of ¼" plywood.
          AB grade which has no knots on
          either side works well. Cabinet-
          quality hardwood, of course, is
          better.
  156 6 × ¾" brass screws
    8 4 × ½" brass screws
   18 8 × 1¼" steel screws
    1 ⅜"-diameter dowel, approx. 1 foot
          Varnish or other finish materials

Instructions

1. Study the plans carefully to get a good idea of how the trays will stack, and how the various pieces relate to each other.
2. Cut out the plywood pieces, preferably with a plywood blade on a power saw. If you don't have one, use the same planer blade you used for the blocks, but put masking tape over the lines you will cut to minimize splintering. Illus. 1.22 shows one way to lay out the pieces on a sheet so that the grain comes out right. Make the first cuts in the order shown. If you have to do this with a hand-held saw or doubt your ability to make an exact cut in a big sheet, make your second cut 19" from the edge and the third cut at 15¾", and make the exact cut on a second pass. (The measurements assume that the saw blade eats up ⅛" or less.)
3. Adjust your table or radial arm saw to cut a 4⅛" strip, and slice off 6 pieces for the side and end pieces of Trays 2, 3 and 4.
4. Adjust the saw to 2⅞" and cut off two more strips for Tray 1.
5. Adjust the saw to 15¼" and cut off all the end pieces and the width of the four bottom pieces.
6. Adjust the saw to 20⅜" and cut the side pieces and the length of the top.
7. Adjust the saw to 18⅜" and cut the length of the bottom pieces.
8. Adjust the saw to 17¼" and cut the width of the top. NOTE: If you can't adjust your saw for these longer dimensions and have to guide material through the saw by

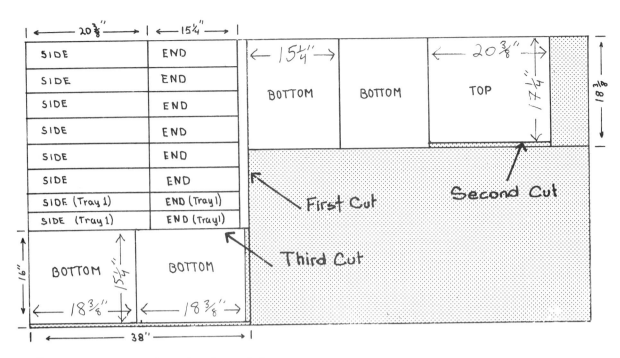

Illus. 1.22   Layout of cuts in plywood sheet

hand, consider tacking the pieces together with small wire nails and cutting them together in a stack, so all will be the same.

9. Cut a 16″ piece off the end of the 1″ × 10″ from which you will make the partition in Tray 4 and rip the rest into 1½″ strips.

10. Cut strips to frame the four bottom pieces as shown in Illus. 1.23, 1.26 and 1.27, using two 6″ × ¾″ screws to secure each piece. The best fit usually results from putting the long pieces on each side first, then cutting the end pieces to fit exactly between.

11. Frame the end pieces of Tray 1 (Illus. 1.24). Again, put the 2⅞″ leg pieces on the ends first, being sure to set them down ⅜″ to leave a niche for the legs of Tray 2. Then measure, cut, and install the top piece between the legs. All pieces get two screws. For a really class act, cut the leg pieces from four separate strips, and set these aside for the next trays so that the grain in the leg pieces of all trays will match.

12. Attach the framed end pieces to a bottom piece.

13. Measure, cut, and attach one framing strip to the top edge of the side pieces of Tray 1, using two screws. (Illus. 1.23)

14. Attach the side pieces to the bottom and end assembly. Use four screws. The two on the ends will go into the framing on the end pieces.

15. Attach the top corners of the side pieces to the ends with one 8 × 1¼″ screw at each end, but countersink the hole with a ⅜″ bit, so that you can drive a bit of dowel in to cover it. Put glue on the dowel, drive it in, then cut it off nearly flush. You can sand it perfectly flush later.

16. Frame the ends of Tray 2 as before, starting with the short vertical legs; however, this time actually line them up in position in the niches on top of Tray 1. This will assure that they fit exactly into the frame of Tray 1. A good craftsman should be able to make all the trays independently and then stack them perfectly in any order, but I have never trusted my own skill enough to risk that. If you assemble the trays in position, at least they will fit in the order they were built in.

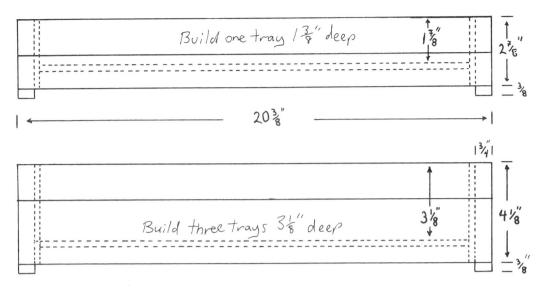

Illus. 1.23   Tray diagrams (side view)

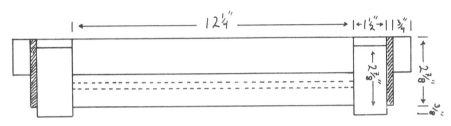

Illus. 1.24   Framed end assembly of Tray 1

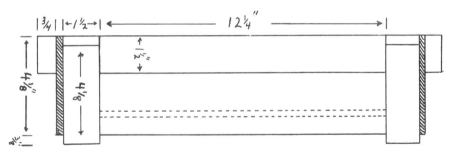

Illus. 1.25   Framed end assembly of Trays 2, 3, and 4

17. When both ends are framed, attach them to the bottom with two screws through the plywood. After attaching the first end, put the second in position so that you will find out if anything is out of line before attaching it.

18. Frame the sides with a single strip as before, and with the end and bottom assembly of Tray 2 in position on top of Tray 1, attach the sides as before.

19. Build Tray 3 and Tray 4 by the same procedure, add the partition in Tray 4 (Illus. 1.26). Cut it from the scrap left from the 1″ × 10″ and secure it with 8 × 1¼″ screws and dowels.

20. Cut pieces ⅜″ × ¾″ × 1½″ thick for "legs" so that the top will stack on top of Tray 4. Obviously, the grain must run the long way for strength. Put them in place in the niches on Tray 4. Then line up the top, and drill for the 4″ × ½″ screws. A bit of glue adds strength.

21. Round off all edges and corners with sandpaper. It is very important to round off the exposed edges of the plywood very carefully; otherwise it will splinter at the

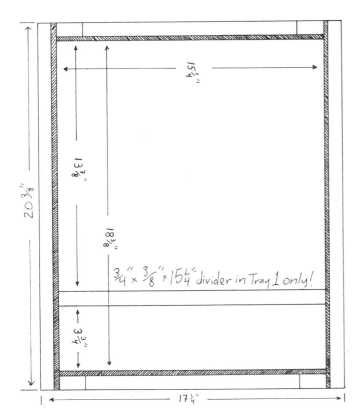

Illus. 1.26 Top view of trays

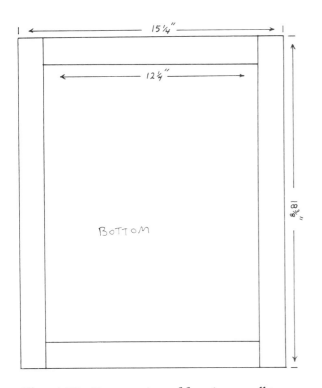

Illus. 1.27 Bottom view of framing on all trays

slightest excuse. Rounding the bottom will also make the trays lock together more quickly and easily.

22. Check to see if the boxes stack in any order. If they don't, put them back in the order where they fit best, and with a soft-tip pen write the number of each tray in the niche at one corner. Then you can always stack them in the same way, and the numbers will be out of sight.

23. If at this point you also notice things that still don't line up properly, consider smoothing over the problem with a belt sander. A little touch here and there can disguise a rather big mistake.

24. Finish as you like. Polyurethane varnish looks good on plywood and holds up well, but any paint shop offers dozens of alternatives.

Before You Build—Reading Project Plans

Real builders have much more flexibility than block builders because they can cut things to fit and order more material when they run short. Many of the block projects represent a good deal of trial and error in finding designs that fit within the number of blocks on hand and the shapes and sizes in the Block Box. No doubt better designs can be worked out, so consider these only suggestions and innovate wherever you see a chance.

In the designs that follow, the block sizes are given by letter and number. The letter tells what shape of block it is, and the number tells what length it is in block units.

The directions that accompany each project use block units. Inch measurements are only used in reference to roof parts or large distances that are easier to measure with a ruler.

Most of the project plans show where to put rubber bands, but do not hesitate to use them elsewhere whenever you need to add a bit of strength.

Read each project through completely before beginning it.

Illus. 1.28 (Opposite page) Detail of Pont Du Gard project

▪ 2 ▪
Bridges

Bridge building is the great test of the engineer, and the record books for the highest, widest, longest, strongest and most beautiful bridges will never close. Our goal is to build them with blocks no more than 9″ long.

Since the first caveman threw a log across an icy stream and crossed dry-footed, builders have invented hundreds of ways to do the job better, so that the history of bridges is really a history of engineering knowledge itself.

Bridges come in every shape, from the simple log across a stream to enormous suspension bridges hung from cables thicker than tree trunks. Wood, vines, rope, stone, metal, cement, and probably many other things have wound up in bridges.

And, because trade, travel, armies, and ideas move slowly without bridges, even the history of a nation may be written in its bridges.

Today, when an engineer stands on the bank of a river or canyon trying to decide how to get his road to the other side, he has several thousand years of wisdom collected by bridge builders of the past to help him, but the questions he asks himself haven't changed much since the time of the caveman and his log.

How strong must it be? How long will it last? What will cross on it? From what should it be built? What will people think when they see it? Will they call it beautiful?

Like model airplanes that really fly, our block bridges don't just look like the real thing, they *are* the real thing, only smaller and cheaper. Building one across a room from one side to the other takes the same kind of imagination and planning and many of the same skills as bridging the Mississippi.

Each bridge in this section has a lesson in it from the history of bridge building. Most of the original bridges can still be seen in Europe or the United States, but their ideas have been copied so many times that anyone who builds them all and learns their secrets will find something familiar in any bridge.

Illus. 2.1　Finished corbelled cantilever bridge with barge passing underneath

Corbelled Cantilever Bridge

This bridge shows the fanciest bridge you can make with plain rectangular blocks. Clearly, this kind of bridge, with blocks simply laid end to end, can't cross a space longer than the longest block. To get more distance across the middle of the channel, blocks were cantilevered out as far as possible (they were made to stick out without the end resting on anything). The weight of more blocks on top holds them in place. That is the "corbelling." Notice that the two corbelled cantilevers balance on the piers. The single block between was put in after the cantilevers were finished. A simple post-and-beam arrangement carries the road up to the main span, as you can see in Illus. 2.2.

The bridge looks good, but it has several problems. It isn't very strong. A toy truck can't roll up and down the steps, and filling them in for a flat road on top makes the whole bridge weaker instead of stronger. The cantilevers also can't be built much bigger before they get very difficult to hold together and keep balanced.

Ancient bridge builders ran into all these problems, and therefore never corbelled any bridges over long distances. They did make some longer bridges from vines or ropes stretched between banks, but these tended to swing sickeningly under horse or wagon traffic. And, sooner or later, people on the bridge got a surprise trip into the river. Timber, lashed or pegged together, made a more solid bridge, but even these eventually fell apart.

Materials

1 Cantilever:
- 28 A8's
- 2 A4's
- 2 Short dowels

1 Pier:
- 16 A4's

Instructions

1. Make the piers of pairs of Block A4, criss-crossed as shown in Illus. 2.3.
2. Start the balancing act of the cantilevers by building upwards with A8's as shown. Insert two dowels to keep the two halves of each cantilever from separating.
3. Put the block that is the connecting point in last, to connect the cantilevers. It can be any length. Illus. 2.1 shows an A8.
4. Put up the post-and-block road on either side.

Illus. 2.2   Detail of post and block road

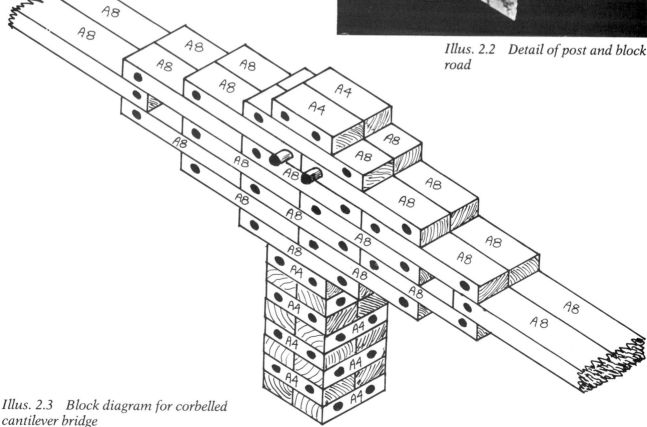

Illus. 2.3   Block diagram for corbelled cantilever bridge

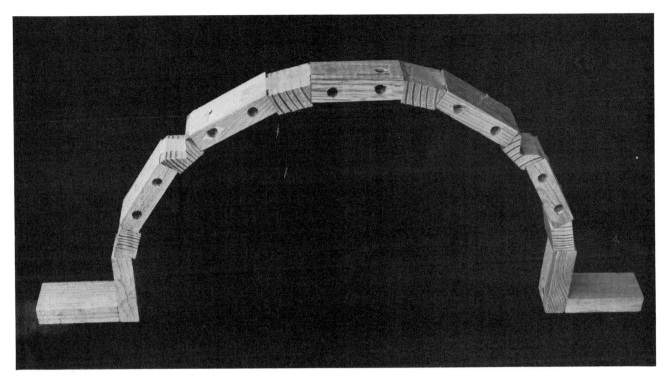

Illus. 2.4   Roman stone arch bridge

Roman Stone Arch Bridge

The weight of a bridge is always trying to squeeze, stretch, twist, or bend the pieces that hold it up. Engineers have to choose materials that can stand the test. Rope, cable, and chain do a good job at pulling, at being flexible and at being stretched and under tension, but are worthless for pushing things or being compressed. Stone is the opposite: It's inflexible and makes a terrible rope, but will take any amount of squeezing or compression. Wood and metal do a little bit of everything, but wood rots, and metal was once rare. Since the Romans needed all the iron they had for swords and tools, and since they wanted material more lasting than wood or rope, they had to build in stone. That meant building in such a way that the stones were only squeezed, never pulled, twisted or bent.

In about 700 B.C., the Romans discovered that stone arches, which only a few builders had ever used before, made strong bridges that would last nearly forever. Blocks cut to fit in an arch would squeeze together under their own weight in the same way. The heav-ier the bridge, the tighter the squeeze, and the stronger the bridge. Of course, the weight on the bridge had to be spread across the whole arch properly, and the feet of the arch could not slide. But, for the engineer, that was part of the job.

The Roman bridges, and most arch bridges since then, were built over wooden frames called "centering." When every stone was in place, the centering was knocked out, and if the job had been done well, the bridge didn't fall.

An extremely good and careful builder might put up most of the arches in this book with the Block Set without anything to hold them together, but it would take tremendous patience. For most of the arches in this book, it is only cheating a little to lay out the arch on its side, tape the pieces together with bits of masking tape, and then lift it into place as one piece (Illus. 2.4). Small bits of tape will not hold against a hard strain, but they allow careful building that doesn't require an extra pair of hands. Notice how the arch blocks are alternated with regular blocks and the place-ment of notched and unnotched arch blocks.

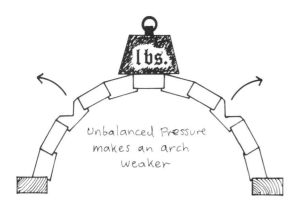

Weight pressing down on the top of an arch that is not balanced by other pressure on the sides will break outwards and fall.

Unbalanced Pressure makes an arch weaker

Weight pressing down on the sides of the arch that is not balanced by other pressure on top will cause the top to pop up, and the whole arch will fall.

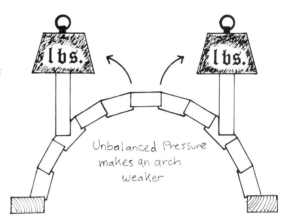

Unbalanced Pressure makes an arch weaker

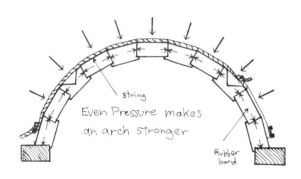

string

Even Pressure makes an arch stronger

Rubber band

Illus. 2.5   Principles of Roman arch bridge construction and demolition

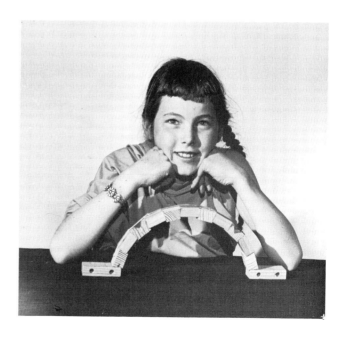

Illus. 2.6   The engineer in this picture also demonstrates the principles of an arch. Elbows, wrists, knuckles, and cheeks all share the pressure and keep her head from falling into her lap.

Illus. 2.7 The Pont du Gard near Nîmes, France

Stone Arch II: The Pont du Gard

The Romans were the greatest builders of the ancient world. Their roads, temples, forts, and palaces may still be seen throughout a good part of Europe and the Middle East. In order to move their armies quickly from one province to another and keep goods moving into their cities, they built the first paved roads ever seen in most of Europe. Good roads, of course, require bridges, and the Romans built many, some of which still carry traffic today. However, the greatest Roman bridge of them all was built to carry water.

In about 19 B.C. a Roman governor of Gaul (now France) with the marvellous name of Marcus Vipsanius Agrippa, ordered an awesome aqueduct built to carry a clear mountain stream into Nîmes to supply several public baths and fountains and the homes of rich Romans. The overflow from that was to flush an elaborate sewer system.

Today, steel pipes can go up and down over hills, so modern engineers seldom have to build anything like the Pont du Gard, but the Romans had to bring water to Nîmes in a ditch that ran *downhill* all the way. For most of its 31 miles it went around the sides of hills or through short tunnels, but the canyon cut by the Gard River posed a problem because it looked as if their ditch would have to go down into it, then *uphill* on the other side. But the high aqueduct that they built sent the water flowing straight across the top.

The Pont du Gard, which means simply "bridge of the Gard" in French, broke records from the start. No stone bridge has ever soared higher, a full 155 feet above the river. The real bridge has six arches on the first level, 11 on the next, and 35 little ones on the top row which is 885 feet long. The biggest

arch jumps 80 feet (Illus. 2.7). And, the whole thing is nothing but a pile of clean-cut rocks. Not a clamp, chain, or scoop of cement anywhere holds it together. For nearly 2,000 years, each perfectly cut block has held up its neighbor by pressure alone.

Why did the engineer build a triple row of arches instead of a single row on top of very tall piers? A block model shows the answer at once. Round arches as long as those in the Gard bridge will simply push over tall piers. By building a row of lower arches first, the engineer had a sturdy platform for building higher. On the piers of the second row he left blocks sticking out from the stonework. They held up the scaffolding and centering that held up the arches before they could stand alone.

A thousand years later, builders discovered that pointed arches like those still seen in churches do not push out so hard against the piers. Those might have made a triple bridge unnecessary, but the Romans didn't know that. Once they had discovered that an arch built around half a circle would stand, they never tried any other shape.

Illus. 2.8 Finished Pont du Gard equipped with pipe for working aqueduct

Materials

Top Deck:
  16 A12's supported by remaining A4's and
     pairs of B4's and B2's

Lower Deck:
  16 A8's
   2 B4's

Middle Deck:
  20 A8's

4 End Piers:
  24 A8's
  40 A4's
   4 B4's

6 Central Piers:
  36 A8's
  66 A4's

Illus. 2.9 Detail of central pier

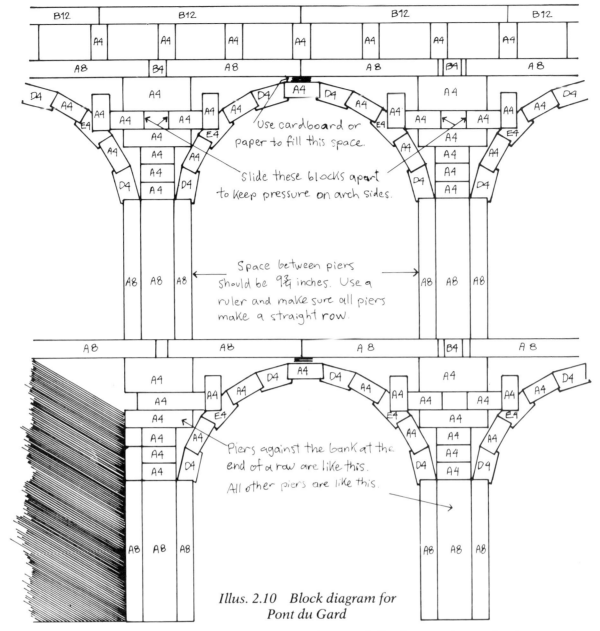

The diagram contains the following labels:

B12   B12   B12   B12
A4   A4   A4   A4   A4   A4

A8   B4   A8   A8   B4   A8

D4 A4 E4 A4 A4 A4 A4 A4 D4 A4 D4 A4 A4 A4 E4 A4 A4 D4

Use cardboard or paper to fill this space.

Slide these blocks apart to keep pressure on arch sides.

A8 A8 A8   Space between piers should be 9¾ inches. Use a ruler and make sure all piers make a straight row.   A8 A8 A8

A8   A8   A8   B4   A8

A4 A4 D4 A4 D4 A4 A4 A4 A4 A4 D4 A4 D4 A4 A4

E4   E4   E4

Piers against the bank at the end of a row are like this. All other piers are like this.

A8 A8 A8   A8 A8 A8

*Illus. 2.10   Block diagram for
Pont du Gard*

Instructions

1. Build the piers by putting 6 A8's around a pair of A10's. Put rubber bands around them; then take out the A10's. See Illus. 2.9. to see how the end piers are made.

2. Be careful to place the piers perfectly straight along a line laid out with a ruler or string, and measure the distance between them carefully. The plans say they should be 9¾" apart. Your Block Set may be a slightly different size, however. Before starting, lay out an arch on its side, tape it, and measure the true distance between the ends.

3. Carefully brace the end piers against the river's banks. Small trunks or cardboard boxes weighted with books make excellent banks for this and the other bridges in this book.

4. Illus. 2.10 shows the best way to build the arches of the Pont du Gard. Notice that in the photograph almost every arch is different (Illus. 2.8). The angles and curves mean that an arch seldom comes out even with the rest of the blocks. After trying many methods, the one shown here in Illus. 2.10 proved best. It needs adjustment at only three places, marked by arrows and instructions.

Illus. 2.11   The Pont St. Benézét at Avignon, France

Stone Arch III:
The Bridge of Avignon

According to legend, an eclipse of the sun in the year 1178 caused a panic in Avignon, France, and while the bishop preached about the end of the world to the terrified people, a shepherd boy ran up and shouted that God had commanded him to build a bridge across the Rhône river. The bishop put him to a test: If he could lift an enormous stone and carry it to the river, that would prove God really had told him to build the bridge. The shepherd boy did it, of course, as easily as if the stone were a large wooden block. And the bridge of Avignon became the longest stone road bridge ever built, nearly 3,000 feet.

All arched bridges ever built before that time had Roman semicircular arches, and since the boy lived not far from the stupen-dous Pont du Gard, he certainly knew about them. Probably many people told him that was the only way to build a bridge, but the shepherd used an entirely new kind of arch in his bridge. The bridge of Avignon has taller, oval-shaped arches that lift the road higher above the stream than Roman arches would, and don't require such thick piers to keep them up. The longest arch spanned 115 feet.

The bridge is very narrow, probably because that made it cheaper and easier to defend if an army should try to cross it. It stood for over 400 years and had as many as 21 arches, although only four still stand. The shepherd, remembered as St. Bénézet, died before it was finished and is buried in a chapel on the bridge. But, assuming the legend is true, he proved that being young and inexperienced should not stand in the way of a good idea.

Bénézet built his long bridge at an angle against the current for extra strength in flood times. Water striking the bridge at an angle would push against it with less force. Also the piers of a straight bridge block the current so water piles up against the bridge. The river hits Bénézets piers one at a time however. Again, flood pressure on the bridge is less.

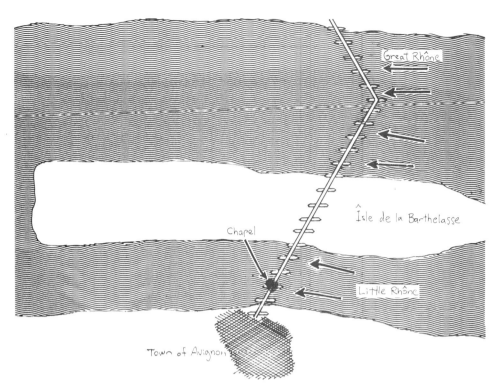

Illus. 2.12   The bridge's original layout (all but four arches have been in ruins since the 17th Century)

Materials
Each Arch:
    2 A4's
    2 A2's
    1 B2
    2 E4's
    4 D4's

Each Pier:
    10 A4's

Road:
    Repeated C8's

Instructions
1. Lay out the arches on their sides on the floor and tape the pieces together (Illus. 2.14).
2. To carry the arches, put pairs of A4's in a line, using the taped arches themselves to measure how far apart they should be.
3. Lift the taped arches into position, adjusting the blocks they rest on so that all gaps between arch blocks close up.
4. Build the piers up to road level as shown in Illus 2.14. (Note that all blocks are doubled as the piers are two block units thick.)
5. Lay the road along the top using thin (C-type) blocks.

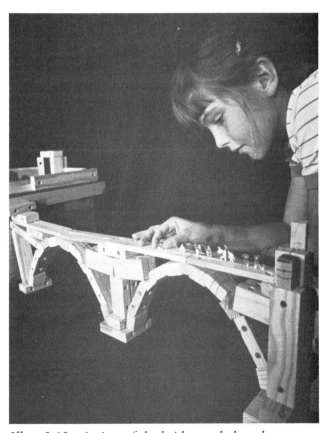

Illus. 2.13   A view of the bridge and chapel

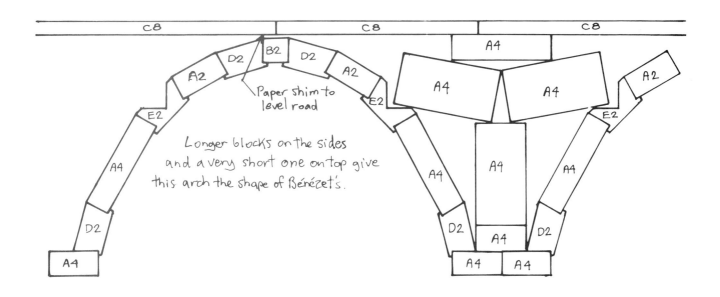

Illus. 2.14   Block diagram of arch and pier

Illus. 2.15   Finished bridge of Avignon

Illus. 2.16   The Ponte Vecchio, Florence

Illus. 2.17   Perronet's bridge at Neuilly, France, was torn down in 1956 to make way for a wider but less elegant modern bridge, but Perronet's idea still survives in many other bridges.

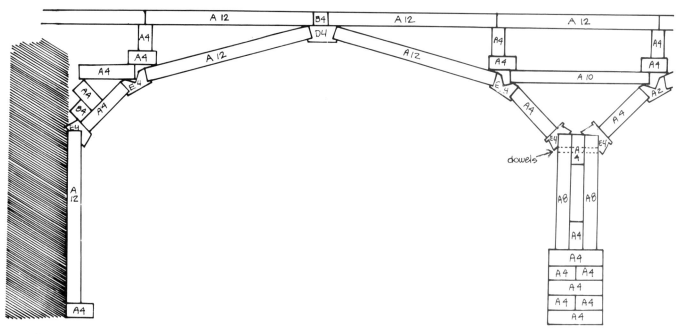

Illus. 2.18   Block diagram for flat arch bridge

Flat Stone Arch: The Ponte Vecchio and Perronet's Bridge

Nearly 200 years after the bridge of Avignon, in 1336 an Italian named Taddeo Gaddi designed the Ponte Vecchio across the Arno River in Florence. The city leaders wanted a *level* bridge between rather low banks. To do that, Gaddi would have had to use a lot of tiny semicircular Roman arches and even more and tinier pointed medieval arches.

Instead, he used a long, low arch. Gaddi knew his flat arches would push outward much harder than Roman arches did, so he built very thick, strong piers that would not fall over as he built his arches one by one. A large number of doubters "knew" the bridge would soon fall, but that was over 600 years ago, and we're still waiting.

Four hundred years passed before a French engineer named Jean-Rodolphe Perronet made the last great discovery in stone-arch bridge building.

He noticed that in a bridge made out of flat arches, the legs of the arches pushed out

against each other. He designed a bridge over the Seine River at Neuilly, near Paris, that had very flat arches resting on very *thin* piers. To keep the arches from pushing over the piers, he planned to build the arches all at the same time across wooden frames, and then knock out the frames all at once so that the arches would push against each other, and not knock over the piers. Once again, the most famous engineers in Europe said the bridge would certainly fall.

Perronet built the whole thing in one summer, because he knew winter floods would carry away his wooden frames. On September 22, 1772, thousands of spectators, including King Louis XV, showed up to watch Perronet's workmen pull out the supports and see the bridge crash into the river.

It didn't.

Notice that the arch in Gaddi's Ponte Vecchio is not a full half-circle, but is *part* of a single, big circle. Perronet's improved bridge, however, has arches that bend down sharply at the ends and make it a very strong and beautiful bridge that many later copied.

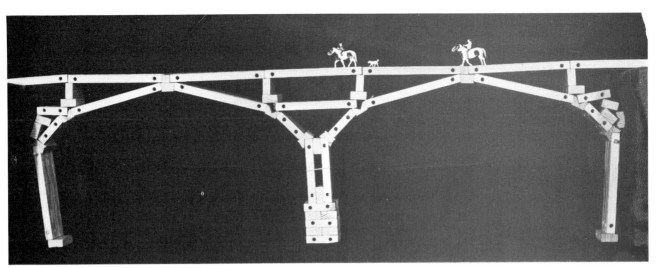

Illus. 2.19   Finished flat arch bridge

Materials

End Piers:
    4 A12's
    2 A4's

Center Pier:
    4 A8's
    12 A4's
    2 Short dowels

Arches:
    8 E4's
    2 D4's
    8 A4's
    8 A12's

Road Support:
    14 A4's
    2 B4's
    2 A10's

Road:
    14 A12's
    2 B4's

Instructions

1. Lay out the arches on their sides on the floor and tape them. Note that the arch is 4 block units wide. The 4-block-unit arch blocks run crosswise and attach to pairs of A12's and A4's. You do not have to tape the arches to the notched arch blocks (E4's) that rest on top of the piers.

2. Set up the piers. (These may be of a different height than shown, depending on the space you need to bridge.) Use a yardstick or other straightedge to get them perfectly in line. Use the taped arches (still lying on their sides) to get the distance between them exact. The piers at the ends are simply pairs of A12's resting on an A4 and leaning against heavy boxes. The central pier could be any combination of blocks of suitable height. Illus. 2.19 shows one made of two pairs of A8's separated by A4's and resting on a stack of A4's.

3. Put E4 blocks on the top corners of the piers as shown in Illus. 2.18.

4. Lift the arches into place. Four hands are necessary because both must go up at the same time to keep the central pier from being pushed over.

5. Build the road supports as shown in Illus. 2.18, and lay the road across the top. If done right, this bridge will support a horse or two.

Illus. 2.20   Finished simple truss bridge

Simple Truss Bridge

Up until the 1800's the biggest and longest bridges were almost all stone arches. The coming of railroads changed that. Trains needed a lot of cheap, strong bridges that could stand the shaking and banging of a heavy locomotive. Also, in the 1800's people learned how to make more and better iron and steel than ever before, and soon put it to work in bridges.

Like wood, steel can stand both pulling and pushing, so it is not surprising that steel bridges often look a lot like old timber bridges. Both are made out of repeated triangles.

Structures with more than three sides are flexible, but the triangle cannot be changed to any other shape.

Hitching together a row of triangles, as the pictures show, makes what is called a truss bridge. It is strong, not too heavy, and easy to build. Really long truss bridges are rare, however, because they have no strength until they are finished. And how do you hold up the end of an unfinished bridge across a mean stretch of water?

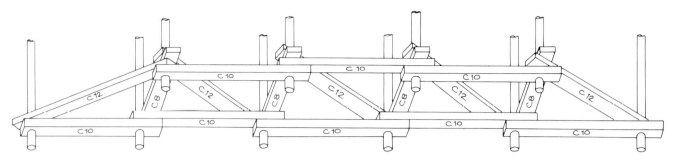

Illus. 2.21   Block diagram for truss bridge

Materials

Each Section:
    4 C10's
    2 C8's
    2 C12's

End Triangles:
    2 C12's
    2 C10's

Each Joint:
    1 Dowel

Instructions

1. The total number of pieces depends on how long a truss you build. Referring to Illus. 2.21, lay both sides of the truss out on the floor. Note that all horizontal pieces are C10's, all vertical pieces are C8's, and all diagonal pieces are C12's.

2. Assemble the truss on dowels according to this sequence of parts. The horizontal pieces go on the outside. Illus. 2.21 shows how the top and bottom rows alternate. The vertical pieces come next to the inside, and diagonals are the farthest inside.

3. To secure all joints, hook a rubber band around the end of each dowel, pull it through the joint around the dowel on the inside and back through the joint, and then hook it around the end of the dowel.

Illus. 2.22   The Quebec Bridge is the world's longest cantilever bridge.

Truss and Cantilever:
The Quebec Bridge

The world's longest leap across open water by a bridge made entirely out of steel triangles—1,800 feet—is made by the cantilever and truss combination that crosses the St. Lawrence River at Quebec.

The engineers built out over the water from stone towers on both sides of the river. By building in both directions from each tower, their webs of steel triangles balanced. These were the cantilevers. This was not an easy trick. On the first try, the whole bridge fell into the river just before it was finished. The engineers had simply made a bad plan, and on top of that did not use heavy enough steel. If they had built a model beforehand with blocks, they would have seen their mistake.

Nevertheless, this weak spot did not show up until work started on the central truss that would join the two ends. Small temporary cantilevers were set up on the ends of the two main ones, and crews on both sides started to build out towards the middle. Each half of the truss would weigh 9,000 tons and a 1,000-ton crane would be run out to the end of the work to lift the steel.

In early August, 1907, the south cantilever began to bend at the weak point, but even then the foreman sent workers onto the bridge. Just before quitting time on August 29, in one great rip, the whole south cantilever went down. Seventy-five steel workers died in the wreck.

The next plan was much stronger, but it too caused fatalities. The central truss was built on shore, floated into position on barges, and lifted up. On the first try, the fastening on one corner broke and the whole thing crashed, killing 11 more men.

Many of the workers, including many of those killed, were Micmac Indians. In spite of the disasters they found they liked the adventure of working on the high steel and it became a tribal tradition. Indian steelworkers have since become renowned for their work on bridges and skyscrapers all over North America.

Illus. 2.23   Finished truss and cantilever bridge

Materials

Cantilevers:
   36 C12's
   16 B12's
   16 C10's
   32 C8's
   32 Dowels 5⅝"–7" (8–10 block units) long

Piers:
   18 A8's

Central Truss:
   4 C12's
   2 B12's
   4 Dowels 5⅝"–7" (8–10 block units) long

Instructions

1. Ideally, the whole bridge, with the exception of the piers, should be built with thin C blocks. Unfortunately, the set does not contain quite enough of them, so you will have to substitute B blocks in a few places.
2. Lay out the pieces for each cantilever: 18 A12's, 8 B12's, 8 C10's, 8 C8's, and 16 dowels.
3. Start with the two B12 uprights at the middle of the cantilever. A dowel connects them at top and bottom. Between these uprights, put the following blocks on the dowel, going from each side towards the middle:
   ▪ At the top: two C12's, then two C10's.
   ▪ At the bottom: two C12's.
4. Secure the joints with rubber bands as seen in Illus. 2.25 and do this for all joints as you build further.
5. Join pairs of C10's on each side of the uprights to C8's, using a single dowel at point A in Illus. 2.24 to make the diagonal braces.
6. Using two dowels and a pair of C10's as uprights at point B in Illus. 2.24, complete the first panel of the cantilever, at the same time adding a C12 and a C8 at the top and a C12 at the bottom to start the next panel. Note in Illus. 2.24 the order in which all these fit on the dowels.
7. Make the next two panels in a similar fashion. Note that you will have to substitute B12's for three of the C12's on each side of each cantilever.
8. Build piers for the cantilevers out of a stack of A8's pinned together with dowels as shown in Illus. 2.25.
9. Balance the cantilevers on top of the piers and tie the "shore arms" of each one to whatever you are using for the banks of the space you are bridging. Chairs, trunks, or boxes make good banks. You must tie down these shore arms, because the central truss, as well as anything crossing the bridge, will unbalance them.
10. Build a short truss according to the plans for trusses in the last project. As you can see from Illus. 2.24, the triangles at each end of this short truss share the dowels at

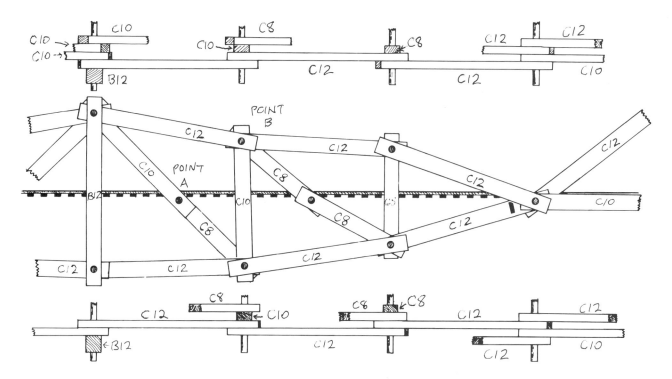

the ends of the cantilevers. Again, the drawing shows the order in which they go on the dowels.

11. You can now lay model train track across the bridge on top of the dowel cross-pieces as Illus. 2.23 and 2.24 show. For a regular road, use strips of cardboard or blocks hitched together as shown in the next project.

Illus. 2.24   Block diagram for half a cantilever. The main drawing shows what blocks to use. The drawings above and below show how the pieces go together if you look down on the cantilever from the top. Notice that the C12's along the top and bottom go on the outside and the different cross braces go on the inside.

Illus. 2.25   Detail of truss and cantilever bridge

Illus. 2.26   Eads's Bridge at St. Louis, Missouri

Steel Arch Bridge: Eads's Bridge

An arch makes a strong and beautiful bridge, but a stone arch is very heavy. A long stone arch is superheavy. And, since no arch can stand by itself until the whole thing is finished, building one over a stretch of moving water full of boats is next to impossible.

But what if you built small trusses that would fit together like the blocks of an arch? Perhaps they would be so strong and yet so light that you could hold up the unfinished arch with cantilevers until the two halves met.

The idea goes back a long way. In about the year 150 A.D., the Roman Emperor Trajan conquered what is now Romania, and to keep in touch with his new lands built a bridge across the Danube River. It had wooden arches 170 feet long, longer than any span built anywhere in the next thousand years. Because stone bridges lasted so much longer than wooden ones, bridges made out of wooden triangles seldom became famous.

Then, in 1867, a remarkable man named James Buchanan Eads decided to try one using steel instead of wood, on a bridge across the Mississippi at St. Louis. Its three 500-foot arches added up to by far the most daring

river crossing ever built up to then. Eads would have admired people who learned their engineering from a pile of blocks on the living room floor. He himself never went to school at all and had never built a bridge of any kind before starting his big one. Many of the best engineers of his time called him ignorant and crazy.

He went right ahead, however, because in the past several of his "ignorant, crazy" ideas had worked very, very well. He had found a way to walk on the bottom of the Mississippi River in a barrel of air to salvage the cargo of sunken river boats. He had found a way to haul the wrecks themselves out of the muddy deep. He had built America's first ironclad warships, and so helped win the Mississippi for the North in the Civil War. In his whole life he had never said "It can't be done."

How Eads built the foundations of his bridge on the bedrock nearly 140 feet below the Mississippi mud was more than half the adventure of building the bridge (see Illus. 2.32). That record still stands. You can't dig that kind of hole in the floor for a block bridge.

The bridge's arch in this book is not as flat or as fine as Eads's. It looks more like one of Trajan's timber arches, but it shows how well the idea works.

Illus. 2.27   Finished steel arch bridge

Materials

Arch:
    38 C10's
    40 C12's
     4 B12's
    26 C8's
    28 Dowels 7" or longer

Road supports:
     7 A10's
    37 A4's
     4 B4's
        Combinations of shorter dowels

Road:
    30 A12's
    16 Dowels 5⅝" long

Instructions

1. The arch is made exactly like the truss bridge, except that every other piece along the top of it is 12 block units long instead of 10 (Illus. 2.29). This will use all the C12's in the set plus four B12's.

2. Notice how the ends are finished with two pairs of C12's on one end and C12's and C10's on the other (Illus. 2.31). If the ends of the arch brace against solid foundations, the arch itself will be extraordinarily strong.

3. The supports for the road are hitched to the dowels in the arch. Illus. 2.31 shows the "knees" constructed at each end of the arch to support stacks of A4's.

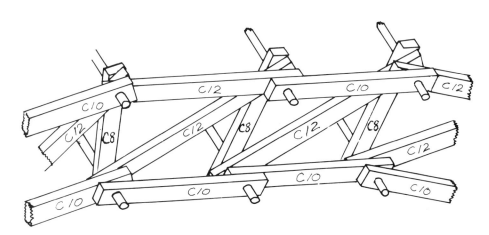

Illus. 2.28   Block diagram of arch

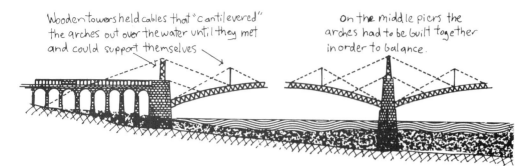

Wooden towers held cables that "cantilevered" the arches out over the water until they met and could support themselves

On the middle piers the arches had to be built together in order to balance.

- Note that one is made from A8's and the other from A10's.
- To the next dowel towards the center from the knees, attach two A10's.
- To each of the next two dowels, attach two A4's.
- To the central dowel, attach three A4's with the dowel running through the wide face rather than the edge, as seen in Illus. 2.27.
- On each end of each "knee," stack up a pile of 6 A4's and one B4, pinning them together with dowels. You don't need one dowel to go through the whole stack: Combinations of shorter ones will do.

4. Construct the road separately on the floor out of A12's hitched together by the dowel-and-rubber-band method shown in Illus. 2.30. Using a pencil point, you can easily push a rubber band in through the hole in the edge of a block and out through the face.

5. Lift the road into place on the supports. This will take four hands. Strips of cardboard on top of some of the supports will help level the road after it is in position.

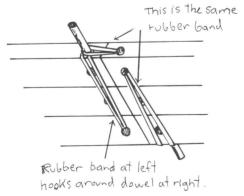

This is the same rubber band

Rubber band at left hooks around dowel at right.

Illus. 2.30   Method for hitching sections of road together

Illus. 2.29   Eads's bridge was the first to be built entirely by the cantilever method.

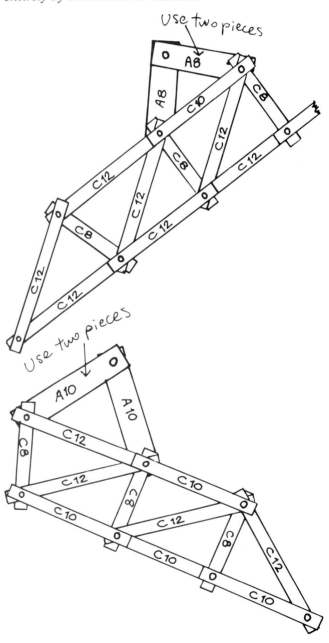

Use two pieces

Use two pieces

Illus. 2.31   Block diagram of the "knees" at each end of the arch

Illus. 2.32   (Opposite page) Coffer dams and caissons

The old way to build stone piers in a river requires a "coffer dam."
The earliest ones were a double ring of logs driven into the mud with
the space between filled with clay. Then the water was
bailed out and workers dug to bedrock,
a dangerous job, impossible in floods.

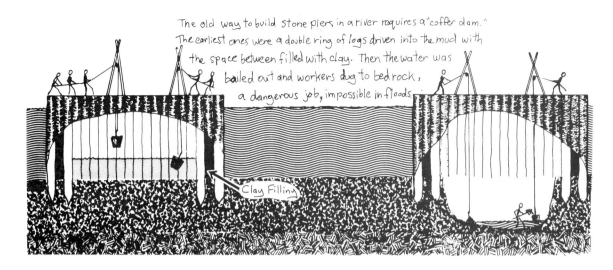

Clay Filling

Where the mud is too deep for digging to bedrock, piles are driven in as far as
possible. Before steam pile drivers, this meant dropping a heavy stone on
a sharpened log. The piles were cut off even, and the stones
were laid on top. Fortunately wood
soaking in water doesn't rot. In time, however,
sand moving with the water will wear it out.

In water too deep for coffer
dams, piers are built on top of
"caissons". The caisson, built of
wood or steel, sits on the bottom like
an upside down cup. Air is pumped
into it to push out the water. Workers
in the caisson dig out the river mud
and as the caisson sinks into the hole
workers on top build the pier higher.

You can hold a glass upside down
in the bathtub and blow bubbles
under it with a drinking straw
to see how this works.

At the Eads' bridge several men
died from "the bends" (air bubbles
in the blood) because they went
from the high pressure caisson to
the outside too quickly.

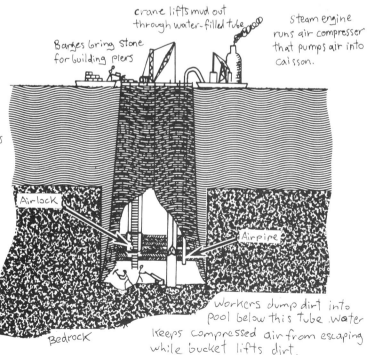

crane lifts mud out
through water-filled tube

Steam engine
runs air compresser
that pumps air into
caisson.

Barges bring stone
for building piers

Airlock

Airpipe

Workers dump dirt into
pool below this tube. Water
keeps compressed air from escaping
while bucket lifts dirt.

Bedrock

Illus. 2.33   The Bayonne Bridge

Steel Arch II:
The Bayonne Bridge

The absolute record for a steel arch is the Bayonne Bridge between Staten Island and Bayonne, New Jersey, in New York Harbor. Completed in 1931, it leaps 1,652 feet across the water, and the roadway hangs from the arch. It is so strong that a 5,000-ton cat can cross it without fear.

Materials
Arch:
   40 C12's
   38 C10's
    4 B12's
   26 C8's
   28 Dowels 7" or longer

Road:
   18 A12's
    3 A10's
    3 A8's
    7 A4's
   14 Dowels 5⅜" or longer

String:
   30 feet of chalkline or similar string

Piers:
   24 A8's (or more if you wish a higher bridge)
   Combinations of short dowels to pin corners

Instructions
1. The piers are made from A8's pinned together with dowels in alternating fashion as shown in Illus. 2.36, but other blocks would do as well.
2. The arch for the Bayonne Bridge is the same as in the previous project's arch except that it has no "knees."
3. Each section of the road is three blocks wide and is joined to other sections as in Illus. 2.38. The road has 6 sections 12 block units long, 1 section 10 block units long, and 1 section 8 block units long. The ends are attached to the dowels at each end of the arch and so keep the arch from spreading (Illus. 2.36).

Illus. 2.34   (Top) Finished block bridge

Illus. 2.35   (Bottom) Another view of the Bayonne Bridge

Illus. 2.36   Detail of pier

4. The strings that hold the road are joined underneath the road by knots that can be tightened to make the road level (Illus. 2.37). This is the taut line hitch, used by every Boy Scout to secure a tent rope so that it can be tightened after the knot is tied. Cross the ends of the string. Take two turns with one of them around the other outside the crossing and one turn inside the crossing. On this last turn, the end tucks under itself. If you tighten these turns carefully, you can slide the whole knot to make the line taut, and it will not slip back.

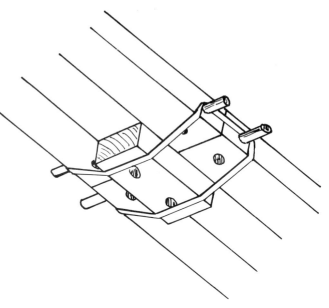

Illus. 2.38   Method for hitching road sections together

Illus. 2.37   The taut line hitch

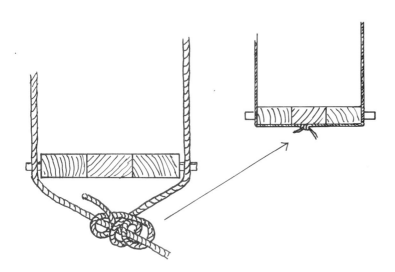

Illus. 2.39   The Golden Gate Bridge in San Francisco

Suspension Bridge: The Golden Gate Bridge

Engineers are always looking for ways to make longer bridges. That means finding a way to build them lighter. Steel arches, trusses, and cantilevers can reach much farther than the old stone arches, but beyond a certain length even they become so heavy and cumbersome that they will not carry their own weight.

Now, it is a fact that a rather thin rope will pull a much heavier load than a rather stout stick can push. In bridge building, that means that pieces that are squeezed must be much bigger and heavier than pieces that are stretched.

The ropes you might use to hang a bridge from the sky will not weigh nearly as much as the props you would need to support the same bridge from below. So why not build hanging bridges?

A Scottish orphan named Thomas Telford who, like John Eads, never went to school, built the first modern suspension bridge. It reached 900 feet across the Menai Strait in Wales in 1821.

The Brooklyn Bridge in New York put the record at nearly 1,600 feet in 1881. In 1931, New York's George Washington Bridge across the Hudson River more than doubled that to 3,500 feet. Then the Golden Gate Bridge in San Francisco stretched to 4,200 feet, and in 1965 the Verrazano Narrows Bridge across New York Harbor reached 4,260 feet. The Humber Bridge in England spanned 4,626 feet in 1981 to win the prize, and even longer bridges are planned.

Illus. 2.40   Finished suspension bridge

The block bridge shown here measures 3,200 millimetres (10.5 feet) between the towers, but it demonstrates all the problems of the big boys. It is tremendously strong, but swings and bounces if something heavy crosses it. A good wind would probably shake it badly.

Engineers have learned the hard way about this fatal weakness of suspension bridges.

After a hurricane nearly blew down Telford's bridge in Wales, a truss disguised as a handrail was built to stiffen the road.

In 1940, four months after it was opened, a 2,800-foot suspension bridge near Tacoma, Washington, began to jump around in a 40-mph wind and finally shook itself down. Trusses were added to several modern bridges for added strength after the Tacoma bridge blew down.

Mathematicians have tried to describe what really happens to a suspension bridge when the wind blows or a heavy weight like a freight train crosses. (In fact, no one has yet risked putting a freight train on a long suspension bridge.) Will the towers bend? Will some parts go up when others go down? Will all the cables get pulled the same way? You can answer these questions nearly as well from your block bridge as you could using the world's fanciest computer.

Materials

Towers:
    32 C12's
     4 B12's
    16 B8's
     4 B4's
     4 A8's
     2 Dowels 8 block units long or more

Road between Towers:
    28 A12's

Cables:
    40 feet heavy chalkline
60–80 feet regular chalkline

Instructions

1. Build the towers of the suspension bridge on the spot where you mean to use them. You may want to build them flat on the floor and then raise them into position, but in fact it is easier to build them standing, just as real bridge towers are built.

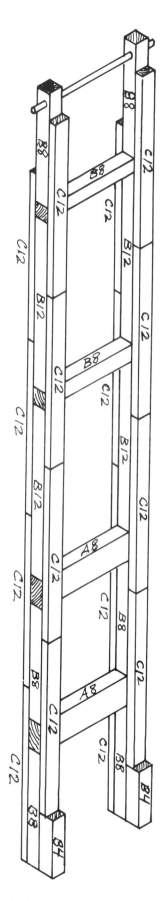

Illus. 2.41 Block diagram of one of the towers

2. As you add each new group of blocks to the tower, putting them in place according to Illus. 2.41, secure them with one or two sets of rubber bands.

3. Lay out a row of A12 blocks on the floor to measure the length of the road between the towers. This could be any distance you want that is a multiple of the A12 block. The model in the illustrations uses 14 pairs of A12's in the main span between the towers. The point is to get the towers exactly where you want them before proceeding.

4. A bit back from each end, you will want heavy boxes of some kind that you can tie the cables to. A box or footlocker full of books does the job perfectly. The end sections of bridge from the towers back to the boxes may be short or relatively long, as space permits. Any string will do, but heavy chalkline or thin clothesline for the main cables looks good. The bridge illustrated here, which was nearly 18 feet overall, took close to 40 feet. The lighter cables that support the road can be regular chalkline, and you will need 60–80 feet of that.

5. Tie one end of each cable to the box, then to the top of each tower by a clove hitch (Illus. 2.43) and make the other end fast to the other box.

6. Make fine adjustments in the length of the cables by sliding the boxes a few inches in or out. Take all the slack out of the section of cable between the boxes and the tops of the towers that you can without pulling over the towers. Whatever the distance between the towers, you must adjust the low point of the cable to 21 block units (15¾″) above the floor. Measure this distance with a stack of blocks or a ruler. If the boxes at the ends of the bridge are higher than that, you can raise the whole bridge by stacking blocks under the towers, and that, of course, will raise the cable also. The weight of the road will not change the curve of the cable between the towers, but it will pull it straight between

Illus. 2.42   Detail of tower

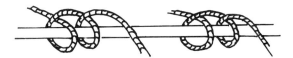

Illus. 2.43   The main cables are tied to the dowel at the top of the tower, like this.

Illus. 2.44   Hang strings from the cable using this knot: a clove hitch finished with a half hitch around the vertical string.

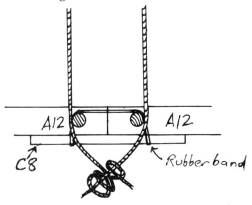

Illus. 2.45   Two strings are tied with a taut line hitch, as shown, to support the road.

the towers and the boxes unless that distance is quite long.

7. Join pairs of A12's for the road with a dowel at each end, and lay them out beneath the cables, but do not join the pairs to each other just yet.

8. For each joint in the road, hang two strings down from each main cable (Illus. 2.44) and join them at the bottom with the taut line hitch shown in Illus. 2.45. By sliding the knot, adjust them to hang approximately 20 block units (15") above the floor. Note that these loops hang side by side from the two main cables and do not pass under the road.

9. Hang the road sections from the loops. Each loop goes around two dowels, one on each of the adjoining sections (Illus. 2.45). When you put in the first section, the cables will sag drastically, but as you add more, it will recover its old curve. Level

the road as much as possible by adjusting the taut line hitches.

10. Finally stiffen the road by looping a rubber band around both dowel ends on one side of each joint, pulling it under the blocks and looping it around the dowel ends on the other side (Illus. 2.45). A C8 block slipped under the rubber bands at each joint increases the stiffening effect.

11. Now readjust all the strings to level the bridge and make sure all strings carry an equal share of the weight.

12. Hang the road sections between the towers and the shore in the same way. The roads leading up to the towers may be as long or as short as you need for your purposes, and can be built with the remaining pairs of A12's and A10's. Unless these are quite long, their weight should not change the position of the main span much at all.

Illus. 2.46   Tower Bridge, London

Drawbridge: Tower Bridge of London

Drawbridges go way back to the time when castles had them to keep out bad guys. Big drawbridges that opened to let ships pass, however, only go back to about 1890. They're a compromise between land traffic, trying to cross the bridge, and a river traffic of ships whose masts are too tall to go beneath the bridge.

One of the first and still the most famous is Tower Bridge of London. It has a truss across the top to steady the towers, and short suspension bridges leading up to the central drawbridge part. Heavy counterweights inside the towers help balance the bridge halves, which until recently were raised and lowered by an ingenious machine powered by the moving river itself.

Materials

Towers:
   42 A8's
    2 A10's
    3 Dowels 5½ block units long
      Short dowels

Truss:
    8 C12's
    2 B4's
    2 Short dowels

Bridge:
    4 A12's
    2 Short dowels

String:
    5 feet chalkline

Instructions

1. Build the towers as shown in Illus. 2.48 from A8's, putting dowels vertically through all the corners. (Single dowels do

Illus. 2.47   Finished drawbridge with tall-masted ship coming through

not have to reach all the way from top to bottom. Several short dowels added together work just as well, as long as *most* of the ends meet inside a block instead of at the joint.)

2. Dowels put in crosswise at points A, C, and F marked on Illus. 2.48 must be specially cut to 5½ block units long to fit into the blocks between the vertical dowels on the corners as shown in Illus. 2.49. (Pencils sawed with a bread knife will do.) They go in as the towers are built.

3. The two 5½-block-unit-long dowels at point A carry the drawbridge halves, which are pairs of A12's joined by a second shorter dowel at the outer ends.

4. The truss that joins the two towers is double-width, which can't be seen in the illus-

trations. Use pairs of C12's separated by a pair of B4's, which will leave a gap for the drawbridge string.

5. Illus. 250 shows how the string raises and lowers the bridge.

- The knots at 1 and 3 are the same taut line hitches used in the last three bridges.
- Knots 2 and 4 may be any good loop knot. A bowline or the taut line hitch will do.
- Tie the end at 4 around the A8 block just above the road in the tower.
- Slide the taut line hitches at 1 and 3 until both halves of the drawbridge stand level.
- Pull the string at 4 to raise and lower the bridge.

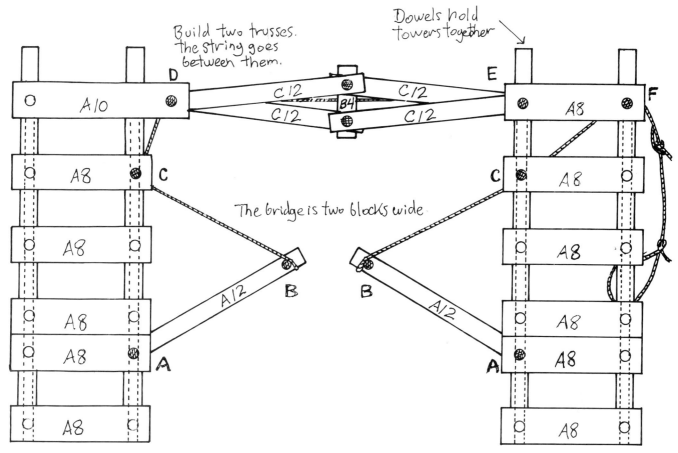

Build two trusses. the string goes between them.

Dowels hold towers together

D   C 12   C 12   E   F

A 10   B4   A 8

A 8   C   C   A 8

A 8   The bridge is two blocks wide.   A 8

A 8   A 8

A 8   A12   B   B   A12   A 8

A   A

A 8   A 8

Illus. 2.48   Block diagram of drawbridge

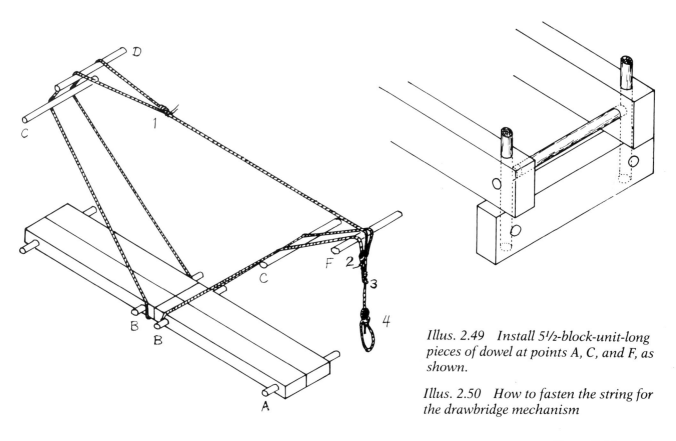

D
C
1
B
B
A
F 2
C
3
4

Illus. 2.49   Install 5½-block-unit-long pieces of dowel at points A, C, and F, as shown.

Illus. 2.50   How to fasten the string for the drawbridge mechanism

▪ 3 ▪
Wheels, Cars, and Things that Move

Illus. 3.1   (And photo on opposite page) Finished train

In all the history of engineering, nothing has been more revolutionary than the invention of the wheel. Cars, trucks, trains, and various machines run on wheels. Because of wheeled things, we also have freeways, railroads, factories, junkyards, racetracks, and a good deal else.

The wheels in the block set, though they look a bit crude, in fact run very well on the dowels, especially if the dowels are greased with a bit of petroleum jelly or candle wax. Two A12's and a B12 with dowels and wheels at each end will make a workable roller skate strong enough to carry a grown man, though such skates wear out rather quickly, especially on pavement. Also, they require something stronger than rubber bands to hold the wheels on.

With a bit of imagination almost anyone can produce a wide variety of vehicles powered by rubber bands, sails, gravity, or a good push. Ramps and tracks also offer many engineering challenges, though, unfortunately, the Block Set does not handle curves very well.

Here are some design ideas that come from things that roll.

Train

In many professions, the experts try to make things ever more complicated and confusing so that they can say, "Maybe when you are as wise as we, you can understand." In engineering, however, the goal is to find the simplest way to do a job, the easiest way to build a machine, and the answer that the most people can understand.

For ten years after the Block Set was invented, many different people tried to build a simple train that could be towed around a living room floor to deliver blocks to building sites or back to the Block Box, but no one found a way to make a coupling that would allow the string of boxcars to go around corners. Meanwhile, enormous temples, palaces, and bridges were built and admired, some of them by highly educated people.

Then one day a kid using the Block Set invented a train that is almost too simple to believe. Any four-year-old can make it. This project is proof that there is always room for a better idea.

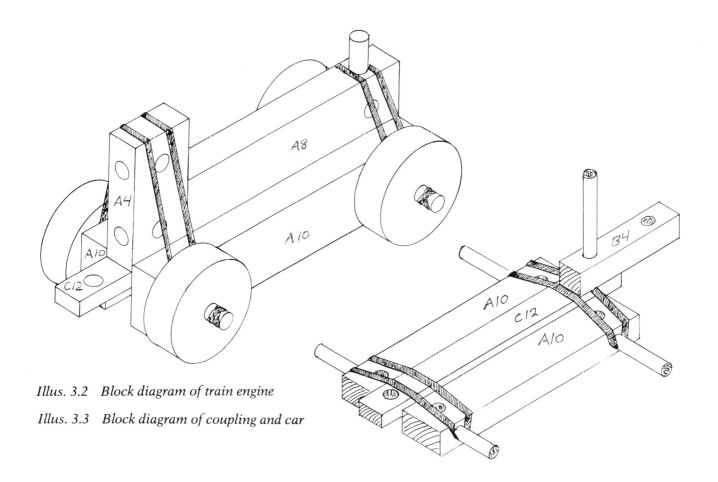

Illus. 3.2   Block diagram of train engine

Illus. 3.3   Block diagram of coupling and car

Materials

Engine:
> 2 A10's
> 1 A8
> 1 A4
> 1 C12
> 2 Dowels 6 block units or more in length
> 1 Short dowel for smokestack
> 4 Wheels

Cars:
> 2 A10's
> 1 C12
> 1 B4
> 2 Dowels 8 block units long or more
> 1 Short dowel for coupling

Instructions

1. The key to making both the cars and the engine of this train is the C12 that sticks out to make the coupling (Illus. 3.2 and 3.3). It sits on top of the dowels put through the A10's and is not really locked into place by anything except the rubber bands. Nevertheless, it stays put very well.

2. To make the cars the A10's are flat (Illus. 3.3).

3. To make the engine, stand the A10's up on edge, and an A4 and an A8 make the boiler and cab (Illus. 3.2).

4. Hook rubber bands around the ends of the dowels and stretch them across the blocks to hold both the engine and the cars together.

5. Put wheels on the engine's dowels and knot rubber bands around the ends of the dowels to keep them on. Wheels on the cars fit the same way, but they are optional. Cars without wheels will slide along quite well.

6. Make the couplings by hitching B4 blocks to the C12's with a dowel dropped down through the holes (Illus. 3.3). It looks as if they would catch in a rug and hold up the train, but that happens only on very shaggy rugs.

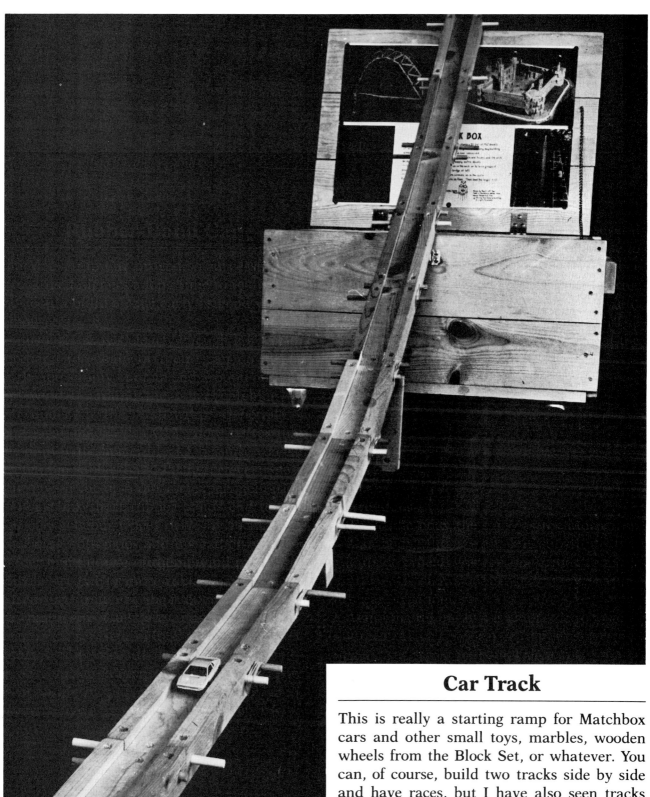

Car Track

This is really a starting ramp for Matchbox cars and other small toys, marbles, wooden wheels from the Block Set, or whatever. You can, of course, build two tracks side by side and have races, but I have also seen tracks built opposite each other so that the racers will crash head-on at the bottom. It is quite interesting to let marbles of different sizes collide, to watch how a large wooden wheel will leap over a small racing car, and experiment with other small catastrophes.

Illus. 3.4   Detail of track joints

Materials

Each Section:
   3 A12's
   2 Dowels

Each Joint:
   1 A4
   1 Rubber band

Instructions

1. The basic plan is very simple (see Illus. 3.5). Each section has two side rails and a central piece. You can, of course, build the sections from blocks of any length. (You can also build them three or four blocks wide for wider vehicles, though that uses a surprisingly large number of blocks.)

2. Illus. 3.5 shows how the sections hitch together with rubber bands around the dowels and how they are stiffened underneath with A4 blocks at the joints.

3. Sometimes the corners of blocks stick out at the joints and snag the passing traffic. To cure that, slip a piece of cardboard or paper about the size of a movie ticket into the joint to cover the corners. Perhaps you can see one of these on page 65 about halfway up the slope.

4. The tricky part is supporting the track from underneath. Stacks of books, sofa cushions, and empty boxes sometimes work better than other blocks to build up the slope.

Illus. 3.5   Block diagram of car track section

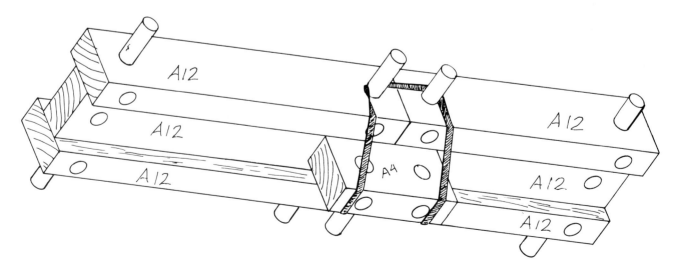

Illus. 3.6 Finished monorail

Monorail

Fortunately, in the true spirit of engineering, someone discovered how to get the job done in a better and simpler way than even the original car track. Why build a fence down each side of the track to hold cars on it, when one down the middle would work as well? Here is an example of a monorail track that works perfectly for cars that use wooden wheels from the Block Set. The wheels roll along each side of the single rail, and the rail guides them.

Materials

Each Section:
>   3 A12's
>   2 Dowels

Each Joint:
>   2 A4's
>   Rubber bands

Instructions

1. Assemble the track like the car track, only arrange the blocks differently according to Illus. 3.7: Two A12's lie flat on either side of a third A12 placed edge-up in the middle.
2. Join the sections by rubber bands that pass under the track and loop around the dowels on both sides of the joint. A4's slipped under the rubber bands on each side of the rail help stiffen the joints.
3. Slope the ramp up with increasingly tall stacks of blocks or books.

The car track just described works very well for small cars. However, building one for a bigger car, or a car with wooden wheels from the Block Set, takes far too many blocks and weighs so much that few care to try it.

Illus. 3.7 Block diagram of monorail section

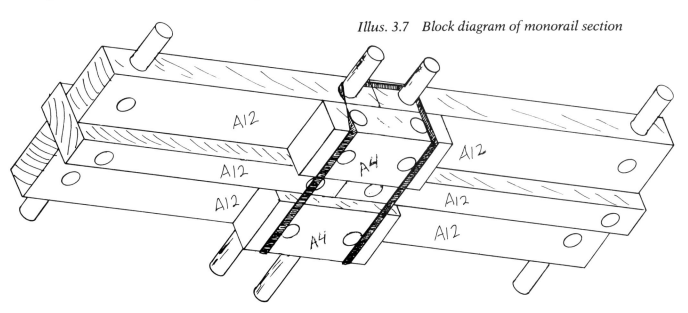

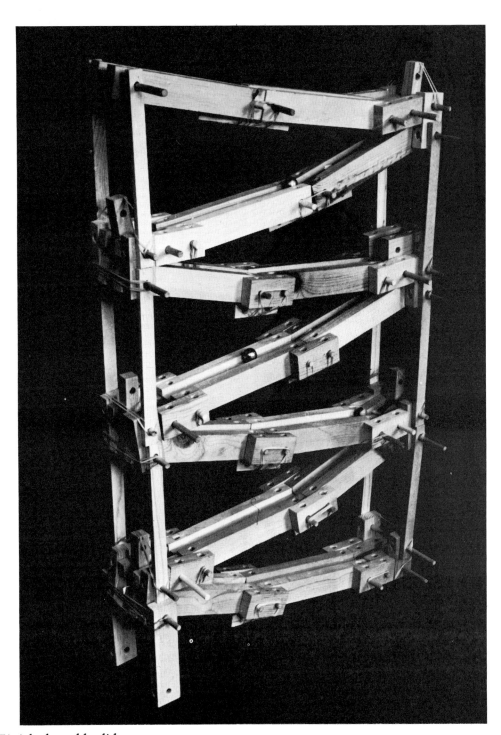

Illus. 3.8   Finished marble slide

Marble Slide

Here is a marble slide that is also just another variation on the car track. Every toy company makes some kind of similar contraption, because two- and three-year-old kids will stay quiet for hours watching marbles whizzing back and forth—zip blop, zip blop, zip blop.

Not surprisingly, adults, teenagers, and many others who don't like to admit it will also spend hours watching marbles go zip blop. In fact a good marble slide seems to come alive when a lot of marbles get going all at once and start making really interesting noises like kazip bladalop, and it's easier to stop eating popcorn than to put the marbles away and do something worthwhile.

Materials

Each Section:
    4 A12's
    2 B12's
    4 A4's
    3 B4's
    1 B8
    7 Dowels

Bottom Legs:
    2 A8's

Upper Legs:
    2 C12's for each level

Instructions

1. Build the main track of each section like the car track, except that here a B12 goes down the middle (Illus. 3.10). Stiffen the joint with a B8, A4 or other block slipped under the rubber bands.

2. For each track section add the end assembly using two A4's, three B4's, and dowels (Illus. 3.9 and 3.10). This will be the lower end of each section when the slide is assembled.

3. At the other end put an A4 on the dowel on each side. This will be the high end, and the two A4's will share a dowel with the low end of the section above.

4. Add A8 legs to the high end of the bottom section as in Illus. 3.8, and secure the joint well with rubber bands. Add C12's to the low end in preparation for adding the next section up.

5. Add the second section to the first. You will have to slip out the dowel at the low end,

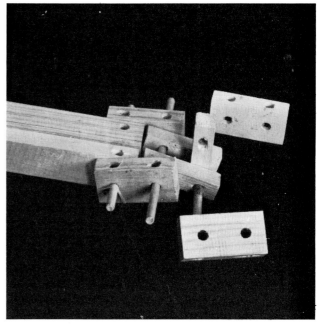

Illus. 3.9   Detail of lower end of track section

rest it between the A4's sticking up from the bottom section, and put the dowel back in.

6. Continue adding sections, using C12's for legs.

7. Stretch rubber bands over the tops of the B4's at the the low end of each section or speeding marbles will knock them over.

8. Try a marble. It may take some adjusting to get all the bumps worked out. In Illus. 3.8, the third track section down has two extra A4's at the low end at right, in order to keep marbles from jumping out, but usually this is not necessary.

Illus. 3.10   Block diagram of track section

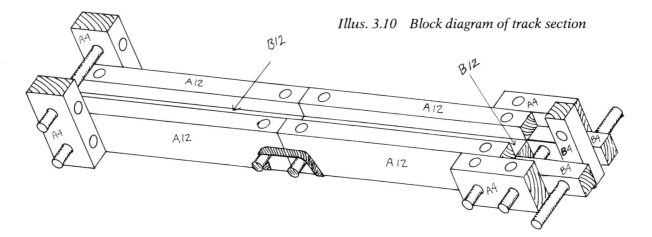

Illus. 3.11   Finished semitruck rig

Semitruck Rig

This design grew from trying to build a train of cars that would hitch together. The hitch is too complicated for a train, but it does make a good truck hitch. In fact, if you hold the blocks together with rubber bands in the right places, this truck will roll as well and stand as much punishment as any wooden vehicle you can buy.

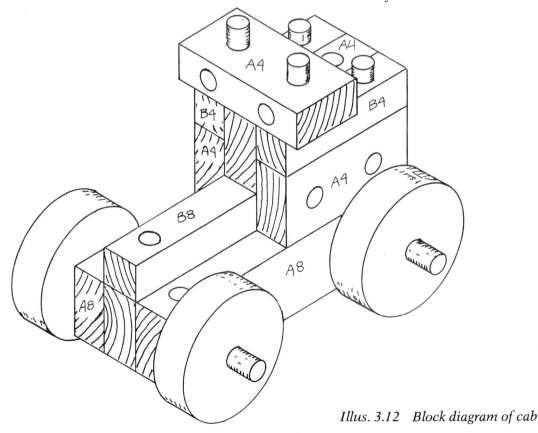

Illus. 3.12   Block diagram of cab

Materials

Cab:

    4 A4's
    3 A8's
    1 B8
    2 B4's
    7 Dowels
    4 Wheels

Trailer:

    5 A12's
    1 A8
    4 A4's
    1 C8
    4 Dowels
    2 Wheels

Instructions

1. Assemble the cab according to Illus. 3.12. Notice how the wheels are held on by rubber bands twisted around the outside of the dowel axles in Illus. 3.11. The other rolling projects have their wheels fastened on in the same way.

2. Assemble the trailer according to Illus. 3.13. The only tricky thing is the A8 that sticks out of the front of the trailer and hitches to the truck. It will swing up and let the front end of the trailer drop to the floor unless you squeeze a C8 or other C block under it. In both Illus. 3.11 and 3.13 you can see the end of this block peeking out.

Illus. 3.13   Block diagram of trailer

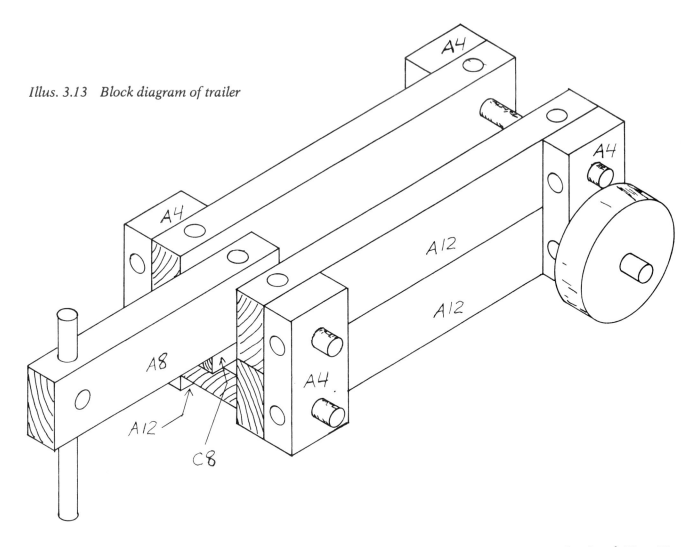

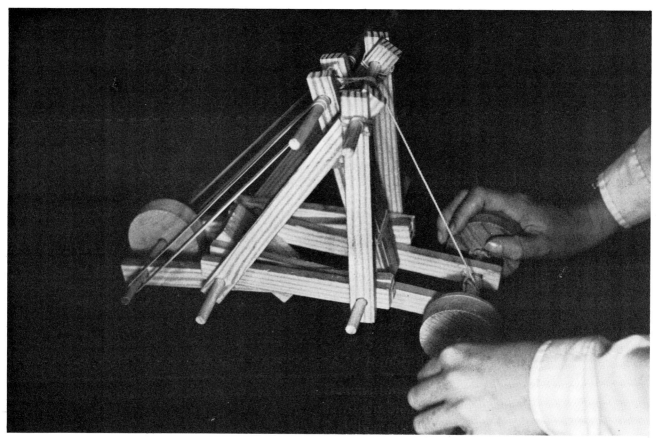

Illus. 3.14   Finished slow car

Slow Car

Of course, if you build toy cars, sooner or later you will want to put a "motor" in one. This is an early design that is terribly complicated, and doesn't work too well, but it's still worth building for three reasons.

- It is pretty amazing to see that a contraption this strange will work at all.
- It has some ideas in it that are useful in understanding many other machines.
- It acts quite differently from most rubber-band toys. The other cars in this book tend to zoom off like dragsters, often spinning their wheels and crashing into things. This one creeps along slowly and powerfully like a huge earth mover. If it only went farther before running down, it would be quite spectacular.

As you can see from Illus. 3.14 and 3.15, the car has both a movable piece and a triangular frame sticking up from it. The moving part (lever) is pulled towards the front axle by rubber bands, and held back by a piece of string that makes a turn around a dowel at the top of the frame and then winds around the rear axle (Illus. 3.16). The engineering puzzle: By adding rubber bands to this moving lever, you can make it extremely powerful—if you use the lever as a catapult, you can shoot the car a long way. But how do you make it release its power slowly?

Because the string passes three times between the lever and the dowel at the top of the frame, the lever in its short trip down has to pull out three times as much string. Notice how much string it takes to pull the lever back. Notice also how much easier it is to pull against the rubber bands with the thrice-wound string than to simply pull the lever back with your hand. This setup works like a set of gears.

Gears, levers, ramps and pulleys all do the same kind of thing. They trade a short hard

Illus. 3.15 Slow car half-assembled

pull for a longer, weaker one or vice versa. In this case, the trade is also seen as a short, fast pull traded for a long, slow pull. The total work done should be the same, but of course friction steals a lot of the energy, and that is the trouble with this car. Even a slick nylon string loses too much power from sliding around the dowels, but the idea is still interesting.

Materials

    1 A4
    1 B8
    6 C12's
    4 C10's
    2 C8's
    3 Wheels
    6 Dowels
    3 feet string
    Rubber bands

Instructions

1. Build the inner assembly shown in Illus. 3.17.
2. Build the outer assembly shown in Illus. 3.18, which has the single front wheel and the moving lever.

3. The inner assembly, with the back wheels, slides up between the legs that hold the front wheel (you have to slide out a dowel to do this). Then the two pieces lock together. On each side C8's hold the two parts in position, giving you the half-finished car shown in Illus. 3.15. In this photo, the moving lever is thrown backwards to show how the parts fit. Flop it forward towards the single front wheel.
4. Next, build the triangular frame out of two pairs of C10's and C12's as shown in Illus. 3.16.
5. The front wheel rotates freely on its axle, but the back wheels must be locked tightly onto their axle so that the string can turn them and make them the "drive wheels." To do this, pull a fat rubber band through the hole in the wheel and cram the axle dowel into the hole alongside the rubber band. Then you may have to trim off the end of the rubber band to keep it from getting in the way.
6. Put two strong rubber bands between the front axle and the top of the moving lever,

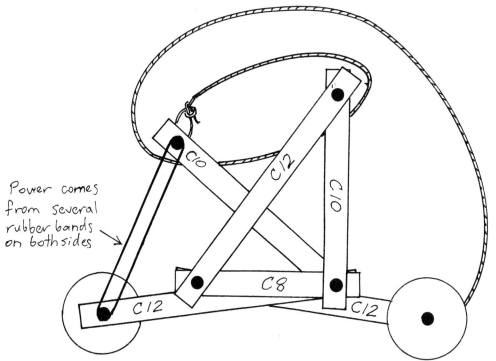

Power comes from several rubber bands on both sides

Illus. 3.16   Block diagram of combined inner and outer assemblies

being careful to keep the tension even on both sides (Illus. 3.16, left). You may want to use smaller rubber bands to hold them in place at either end of the lever's dowels.

7. Tie a string, preferably nylon cord, to the middle of the moving lever's dowel and pass it around the top of the frame as shown in Illus. 3.16. Then tighten the string and draw back the moving lever.

8. At this point, it is helpful to have a friend hold back the power lever while you wrap the string around the rear axle, being careful to catch the end under the first few turns. Keep winding until the string holds the power lever all the way back.

9. Finally, let her rip.

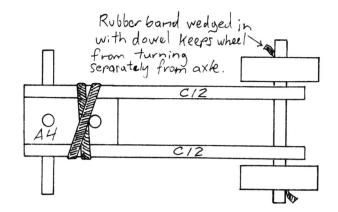

Rubber band wedged in with dowel keeps wheel from turning separately from axle.

Illus. 3.17   Block diagram of inner assembly

Illus. 3.18   Block diagram of outer assembly

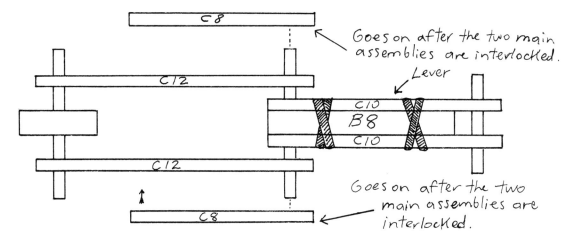

Goes on after the two main assemblies are interlocked.

Lever

Goes on after the two main assemblies are interlocked.

Illus. 3.19   Finished mousetrap car

Mousetrap Car

Many schools hold an annual competition called Odyssey of the Mind, in which contestants have to solve various engineering problems with simple materials. One year, the challenge was to build a car powered only by a mousetrap that would cover the most distance on one wind.

This contest brought into existence an enormous number of very different designs with wheels and axles of different sizes and all kinds of additions to the mousetrap itself. Generally, the simplest and lightest did best.

The design here is no champion because the wood is too heavy and the friction in the axles too great, but it does better than many over-engineered entries that took a lot more effort to build. It goes together very easily and will really scoot across a linoleum floor.

If you get into racing these cars, you will want to experiment with putting the mousetrap closer to or farther away from the axle that it turns. You can wind it to go in either direction. You can also lash on dowels or pencils to extend the trap itself so that it makes a longer sweep when it closes. This allows you to wind more string around the axle, but you will have to find out for yourself whether it improves performance.

On some floors rubber tires help traction. They are easily made from our Block Set wheels by putting fat rubber bands around the rims of the driving wheels. Note also that the driving wheels are again locked on the axle by a rubber band put through the hole before the dowel is pushed into it.

One definite improvement that would be cheating in a formal contest is to wind rubber bands instead of string around the axle. You will have to experiment with size and number, but they should be long enough to start winding before the trap is set. Wind until they are stretched as tight as possible before you do set the trap. Then wind some more. Such a car will easily run the length of a basketball court.

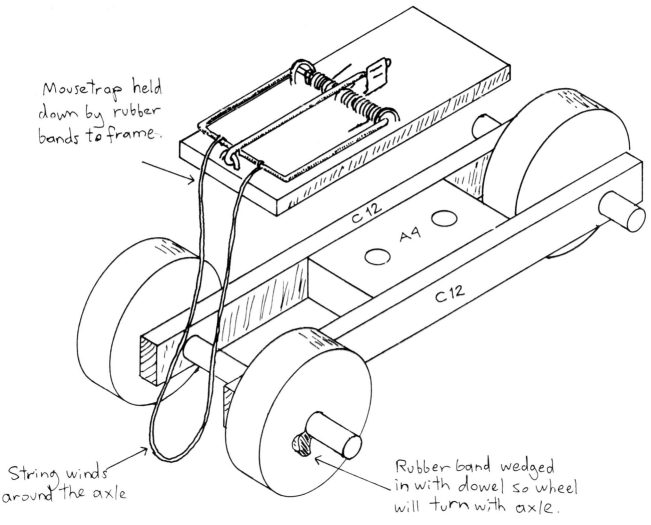

Mousetrap held down by rubber bands to frame.

String winds around the axle

Rubber band wedged in with dowel so wheel will turn with axle.

Illus. 3.20   Block diagram of mousetrap car

Materials
1   A4
2   C12's
2   Dowels
3   Wheels
8" String
   Rubber bands

Instructions
1. Assemble car according to Illus. 3.20.
2. When putting on the wheels, wedge rubber bands into the holes in the wheels as the dowels are put in. Now the wheels will be driver wheels instead of loosely spinning wheels.
3. Hold the mousetrap to the frame with rubber bands. Cock the mousetrap in open, about-to-be-sprung position.
4. Take the string tied to the mousetrap bar and wind it around the axle.
5. Spring the mousetrap.

Illus. 3.21   Finished rubber-band car

Rubber-Band Car

The Mousetrap Car proved so successful that it took its designers a long time to realize that they could build a car nearly as good without a mousetrap.

Illus. 3.21 shows clearly enough how a rubber band (or chain of them) can do all the work. You simply knot an end around one axle and wind it around the other, catching the end under in the first wrap. Generally, a longer car made with C12's does better than one built with shorter blocks, because you can stretch the rubber band farther. Nevertheless, you have a lot of room for experimentation. You can link short rubber bands end to end. You can get four-wheel drive by locking the wheels on both axles and instead of tying the rubber band to one of them, wind it on both. You can try two or more rubber bands side by side, or try stretching the rubber bands all the way out before you start winding.

One quite successful scheme uses several short, strong rubber bands tied side by side to the idle axle with longer, weaker rubber bands tied to those. When you wind the car, the weaker bands will stretch all the way out before the short strong ones stretch at all. The short ones give the car a burst of energy at the start. Then the long ones take over.

Materials
    1 A4
    2 C12's
    2 Dowels
    4 Wheels
    Rubber bands

Instructions
1. Build the body the same as the Mousetrap Car body (Illus. 3.20), but substitute two outside wheels for the one central wheel. Illus. 3.21 shows rubber-band tires that increase traction.
2. Wind the rubber bands from axle to axle.

Marionette

Probably every engineer sooner or later dreams of building the ultimate machine, a robot that performs as well as a human being. The ancient Greeks claimed that the same Daedalus who built the maze of King Minos of Crete also built a mechanical policeman out of bronze who marched around the island breathing fire and arresting people.

This marionette, however, is a very pleasant human character that can perform wonders in the hands of a good puppeteer.

Materials

Marionette:
    2 A4's
    6 B4's
    6 C12's
    2 C10's
    7 C8's
    3 Long dowels
    6 Short dowels
       Rubber bands
       Sock for head
       Paper or cloth hands

Body Controls:
    4 C12's
    1 C10
    2 C8's
    1 Short dowel
    1 Long dowel
       String

Instructions

1. Assemble the marionette according to Illus. 3.24. The head is made of a sock stuffed with rags. The face is embroidered on. It is held onto the body by rubber bands. The hands are of paper or cloth. Attach them with rubber bands as shown in Illus. 3.24.

2. Use short dowels with rubber bands twisted around the ends to make loose joints at elbows and knees. Naked, these joints have an annoying way of hanging up on each other and the strings, but if you can put your wooden friend in trousers, all goes well.

3. The frame for controlling the strings is the sophisticated design used by professional puppeteers and takes some practice to use (Illus. 3.23). As Illus. 3.22 shows, the top bar that controls the hands separates from the rest of the frame for reaching gestures.

Illus. 3.22   Finished marionette

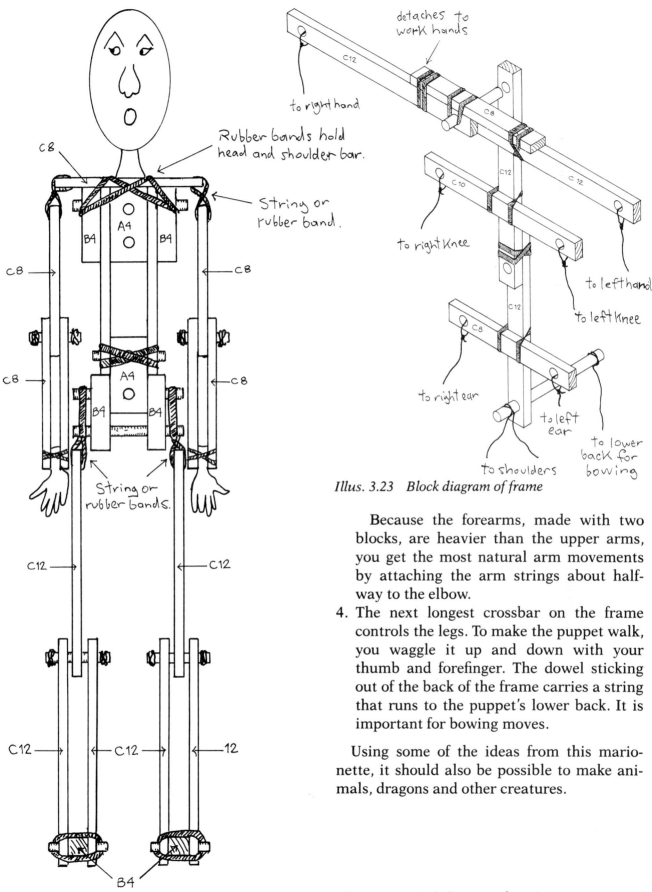

detaches to
work hands

to right hand

C12

C8

Rubber bands hold
head and shoulder bar.

C8

String or
rubber band.

B4   A4   B4

C8   C8

C10

C12   C 12

to right knee

C8   C8

B4   A4   B4

to left hand

to left knee

C12

String or
rubber bands.

C8

C12   C12

to right ear

to left
ear

to shoulders

to lower
back for
bowing

C12   C12   12

B4

Illus. 3.23   Block diagram of frame

Because the forearms, made with two
blocks, are heavier than the upper arms,
you get the most natural arm movements
by attaching the arm strings about halfway to the elbow.

4. The next longest crossbar on the frame
controls the legs. To make the puppet walk,
you waggle it up and down with your
thumb and forefinger. The dowel sticking
out of the back of the frame carries a string
that runs to the puppet's lower back. It is
important for bowing moves.

Using some of the ideas from this marionette, it should also be possible to make ani-
mals, dragons and other creatures.

Illus. 3.24   Block diagram of marionette

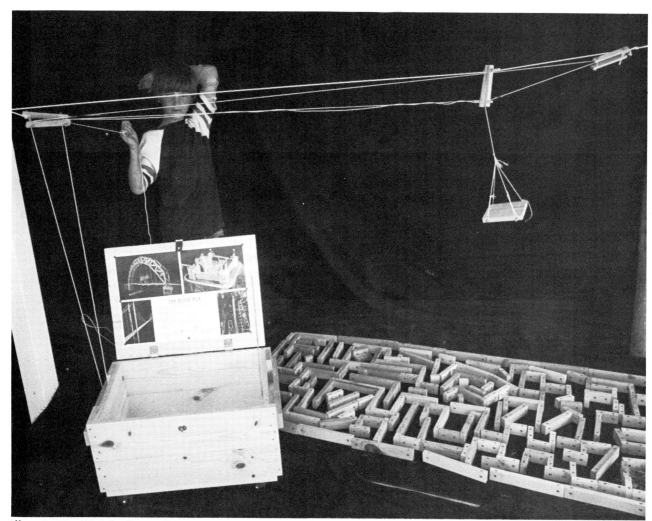

Illus. 3.25   Finished travelling crane over construction work

Travelling Crane

Factories and large building sites usually have some kind of machine for moving steel, timbers, brick, and cement. A crane like the one here that moves overhead along a track or cable is called a travelling crane. This one will not move blocks nearly as fast or as well as you can do it by hand, but it somehow makes the job seem more important.

Materials

    6 *C8's*
    6 *Short dowels*
    6 *Rubber bands*
    Cord

Instructions

1. First, find a way to stretch the main cord over the workplace. It has to be anchored very strongly at both ends. Don't tie it to a bookshelf, chair, or lamp that might fall over, or a light bracket that might pull out of the wall. Windows often have places to tie to, or you can tie the string around a block and close the window over it. Door hinges and door knobs also work if closing and opening the door doesn't upset things.

2. Make three pulleys out of two C8's connected top and bottom by short dowels with rubber bands looped around the ends to keep them from sliding out (the same method used to keep wheels on the car models).

3. Set one of the pulleys to slide back and forth freely on the main support string. The others are tied at each end as shown in Illus. 3.26, top.

4. The "back-and-forth" string ties first to the sliding pulley, goes over one of the end pul-

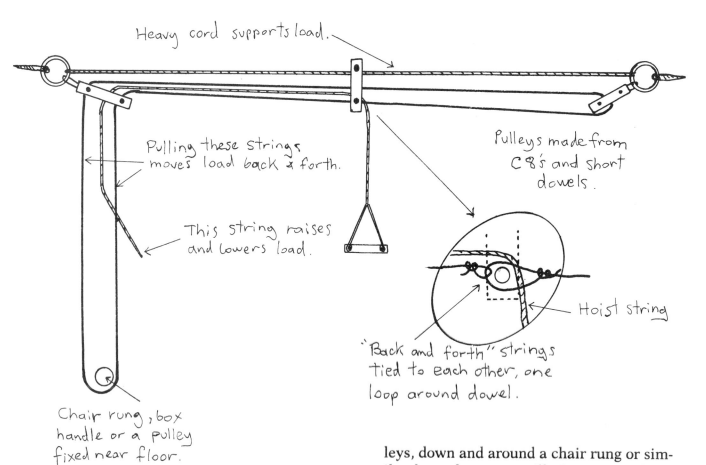

Heavy cord supports load.

Pulling these strings moves load back & forth.

This string raises and lowers load.

Pulleys made from C8's and short dowels.

Hoist string

"Back and forth" strings tied to each other, one loop around dowel.

Chair rung, box handle or a pulley fixed near floor.

Illus. 3.26   Diagram of travelling crane

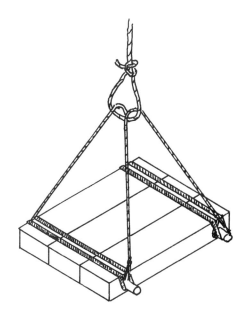

Illus. 3.27   Example of a lifting rig

leys, down and around a chair rung or similar bar where you will sit to control the crane, then back up over the end pulley, all the way across to the other end pulley, and back to the sliding pulley (Illus. 3.26).

If you have it right, you can sit where the "back-and-forth" string goes around the rung and make the sliding pulley go back and forth by pulling one string or the other.

5. To raise and lower loads you need one more string that runs up over the end pulley, out to the sliding pulley, and down to the load.

6. Illus. 3.27 shows a good rig for lifting blocks. For other work you might just want a hook. If you do that, you can tie a block to the string just above the hook in order to give it weight so that it will go up and down without a load.

· 4 ·
Castles, Palaces, and Temples

Except for ants, bees, beavers, and prairie dogs, probably no creatures spend more time and effort than humans on building places to live, work, and play. No one knows exactly when people got tired of looking for good caves and decided to build their own homes, but it happened tens of thousands of years ago, and since then they have invented an extraordinary variety of ways to build them.

Most people who mess around with blocks start building houses just as surely as a beaver will start gnawing trees, but unlike beavers we build for sports, recreation, worship, and other reasons besides shelter and protection. The plans in this section show a small bit of the human experience of the last 10,000 years or so, and may perhaps open the door to any number of new ideas.

Castles, Palaces, and Temples • 83

Illus. 4.1   The Great Pyramid Complex and Sphinx at Giza

Pyramid

The pyramids of Egypt are without doubt the most famous piles of blocks ever put together by mankind. They are also among the largest and oldest. The first big one, built nearly 5,000 years ago for King Zoser, rises 200 feet above the desert. The architect, Imhotep, is also the first architect whose name we know.

A hundred years later, a Pharaoh named Khufu built the Great Pyramid at Giza, 480 feet high, out of about two million blocks. It still holds the record as the world's most massive stone building.

The Pharaohs believed that they would become gods after death but that they couldn't do much on Earth in the afterlife unless the spirit and soul could find and recognize the earthly body. To make sure of that they had themselves mummified, and they built the pyramids as conspicuous but hopefully robber-proof tombs.

Many scholars have speculated on why the pyramid builders arranged things as they did, but all agree that the shape they chose has a certain beauty and power to it. Pyramids have the interesting characteristic that they change shape as you walk around them. The sides of the ones at Giza slope up at the fairly steep angle of about 52°, but you see that angle only when facing the middle of one side. Seen from the corner, the edges slope up at a **much** flatter 42°. Thus, every view looks different, and as works of art the two dozen or so Egyptian pyramids never become boring.

Illus. 4.2 Finished pyramid with river-bank temple

According to ritual, dead Pharaohs were brought up the Nile to a temple at the water's edge where the priests embalmed the body. Then it was taken up a covered passageway to another temple built against the east face of the pyramid itself for more rites and prayers. That temple looks as if it should be the opening to the burial chamber itself, but it in fact marks a false entry, perhaps to fool grave robbers. The mummified body was actually brought in through a secret entrance on the north side.

After laying it to rest in a sarcophagus cut from a single stone in the very heart of the pyramid, the priests pulled out wooden props that let great stone slabs drop down to block the passage and sealed it over from the outside, hoping to hide the entrance forever. But, thieves and archaeologists eventually found the hidden passage.

With less than a million or so blocks, you cannot build anything as sophisticated as the Great Pyramid at Giza, but building a small one will demonstrate how complicated such a

Illus. 4.3   Pyramid base

The pyramid here, with a base 26 block units square, contains 3,278 cubic block units in 14 layers. Two more layers, 28 and 30 block units square respectively, will bring the total to 4,962 cubic block units. That is the limit, because the whole Block Set only contains 5,280 cubic units.

Building the biggest, most beautiful pyramid possible is a challenge you will have to work out for yourself.

Instructions

1. Build a square base, being careful to count the units on each side. Illus. 4.3 shows a base 26 block units square. Notice that in this case you have to fudge a bit with half-unit (C) blocks to get the secret passage to the tomb exactly in the middle. This is easier if the base has an odd number of block units, but then building the upper layers becomes a little messier. Again, the choice is yours.
2. Lay out in the first layer the secret passage and the burial chambers, using A blocks set on edge.
3. Build the second layer, two block units smaller than the first (if you want the same slope as the pyramid here). This will come to the top of the walls around the passage and burial chambers. The next layer, again two block units smaller, will cover them. Keep building successively smaller layers until you reach the top.
4. Build the temple at the false entrance, the river bank temple, and the connecting passage. Illus. 4.2 shows one idea for this. The folded paper boats are very similar in shape to the ones that actually brought a Pharaoh's body up the Nile in ancient times.

simple geometric shape can be, and the astonishing number of blocks it requires.

Our pyramid is not as steep as the ones at Giza. Each layer goes in one block unit and up one block unit, which makes the faces slope 45° and the edges about 35°. With a little more difficulty and quite a few more blocks, you can make each layer go in ½ block unit for every step up. That makes a steeper 63° slope.

You can arrange blocks in an infinite number of ways inside a pyramid, using thousands of combinations of blocks. Rather than trying to repeat the single possibility that happens to be pictured here, look at the problem, as Pharaoh's engineers had to, from the standpoint of how many blocks you can bring to the site and stack before Pharaoh dies.

Illus. 4.4   Minoan Palace of Knossos in Crete

Minoan Labyrinth

In ancient Greek legend, Minos, king of the island of Crete, imprisoned the Athenian inventor Daedalus and forced him to build an incredible palace at Knossos. King Minos had some unique building requirements because his wife had given birth to a half-man, half-bull creature called the Minotaur that ate only human flesh. To house this monster, Daedalus constructed a maze in the basement so complicated that unlucky people could get in, but neither they nor the Minotaur could find the way out. King Minos forced surrounding nations to supply young men and women to feed his weird stepson.

Finally, a hero named Theseus sailed to Crete as one of the victims of this hideous tribute and managed to kill the Minotaur, although not without aid from Daedalus, and Minos's daughter Ariadne. They gave him a ball of thread to help Theseus find his way through the maze and out again.

For well over a thousand years, no one believed the myth had any truth to it. Then, in 1900, an English archaeologist named Sir Arthur Evans began to dig in the ruins of Knossos on Crete to see what evidence he could find of the old story. At that time, the ruins were mostly piles of rock drifted over by blowing soil, and though well known, no one knew if they were Greek or Roman. They turned out to be a vast palace built in a style all its own by people whose language and civilization differed from any other then known. The earliest levels of the palace dated back to 2,000 B.C. and it had obviously been the seat of powerful rulers up to about 1450 B.C.

The vast number of storerooms, halls, passages, and chambers could easily have started the legend of the Labyrinth. Since the palace was built long before the Greeks built anything nearly so complicated, it is easy to believe that a Greek prisoner stumbling around the bottom floors of the palace by the light of a flickering torch might invent some powerful

Illus. 4.5   A modern reconstruction of the Minoan labyrinths

tales. Furthermore, paintings on walls and pottery show both men and women athletes turning handsprings over the horns of charging bulls.

How many visiting foreigners died trying this local sport is not known, and it is not known if Minos or any other rulers at Knossos demanded slaves from other countries, but they must have feared no enemies because the palace had no fortifications or defenses whatever.

Building the palace of Knossos out of blocks would be quite an undertaking, even if we knew exactly how it looked 3,500 years ago.

Blocks, however, can make a fantastic labyrinth. The one in Illus. 4.5 was constructed for mice. The builders took a sliding patio door off its tracks and covered the maze to keep their rodent minotaurs from escaping or cheating.

The two mice explored vigorously, and soon knew the whole layout perfectly. It would have been interesting to have given them some nesting material and grain and kept them there a few days to see which chamber they might settle in and where they would store their food.

Illus. 4.6   The Temple of Aphaea at Aegina

Greek Temple

A lot of buildings grew in a haphazard way, tower by tower, wing by wing, according to the owner's money and imagination and need. This was not true of Greek temples, which were highly stylized. The Greeks believed in gods who behaved, looked, and thought very much like regular people. To honor these gods, the Greeks built them fine houses in conspicuous places. It didn't matter if these temples were small and dark inside, since the god's statue, if there was one, didn't need much light or space. Animal sacrifices, the feasting that followed, and other ceremonies took place outside, so the important thing was to build a house that looked perfect from the outside and made a nice background. That honored not only the god but also the community that built such a fine temple.

The first temples, built sometime before 800 B.C., were rather simple rectangular wooden buildings, and for the next 500 years the basic plan was not changed. The Greeks just took the original form and tried to make it perfect. Early on, they switched from wood to stone. Then they worked on the shape, the style of columns, and other details too numerous to mention.

The Parthenon in Athens, begun in 447 B.C., is considered perhaps the most perfect building ever built. Even in ruins it still looks beautiful from all sides. Almost every major city in the western hemisphere has buildings that copy some part of it.

The ancient Greeks spent a great deal of time thinking about beauty, and they looked hard for natural rules that explain why one thing pleases the eye and another doesn't. When they had to decide how high and how wide, they reasoned that since tall and skinny

Illus. 4.7   Finished Greek temple

and short and fat both look ugly, a perfect shape must lie somewhere in between. Likewise columns put too close together look cluttered and unnecessary, while too far apart they look stringy and weak, so there must be perfect spacing in between.

In some cases, the Greeks actually decided that they had to cheat to make things *look* perfect. They noticed, for instance, that columns cut perfectly straight *looked* pinched in the middle, so they made them bulge slightly in the middle. Perfectly upright columns also seemed to lean out a bit, but Greek columns look straight because they actually lean in slightly. The Greeks also found that a perfectly level floor appears to sag a little. Their best temple floors, however, look flat, because they in fact curve up ever so slightly.

You can't get that persnickity with our blocks, but the temple here is modelled after a real one, the temple of Aphaea at Aegina built around 490 B.C. (Illus. 4.6). Building it meant thinking through many of those questions of how high, how wide, how far apart, how many, how steep, etc. Many Greek builders tried to find a simple "perfect" rule and use it again and again, so that even the blocks in the wall had the same "perfect" shape as the temple itself. You get some feel for what that means as you build with wooden blocks that were all cut beforehand, also according to a rule.

Materials

Platform:
> 6 A12's
> 6 A8's
> 92 A4's

Steps:
> 4 C12's
> 2 C10's
> 8 C8's

Columns:
> 22 A10's
> 14 A8's
> 14 A2's (or pairs of B2's)

Blocks on Top of Columns:
> 16 A12's
> 8 A8's

Inside Temple Walls:
> 7 A12's
> 36 A8's
> 22 A4's
> 12 A2's (or pairs of B2's)
>> Dowels in combinations to pin walls
>> together

Colonnade around Statue:
> 4 B12's
> 14 B8's
> 12 B4's

Blocks over Interior Columns:
> 8 B12's

"Pediments" over Gables:
>> Cardboard with pictures

Roof:
>> Cardboard, preferably corrugated on
>> one side

Beams across
the tops of columns

Corner columns
have C10's
on both sides.
instead of a C12

Making all 36 columns
will require using some
combinations of A8's
plus an A2 in place
of the A10.

C12 A10 C10

This piece
slides up so
rubber bands
can catch at
the top.

Detail showing how
columns attach to the
lintel blocks. Note the
overlap at the corner.

Illus. 4.8   Detail of columns

Illus. 4.9   Detail of lintels

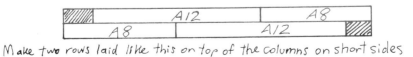

Make two rows laid like this on top of the columns on short sides

Make two rows of blocks laid like this on top of the columns on long sides.

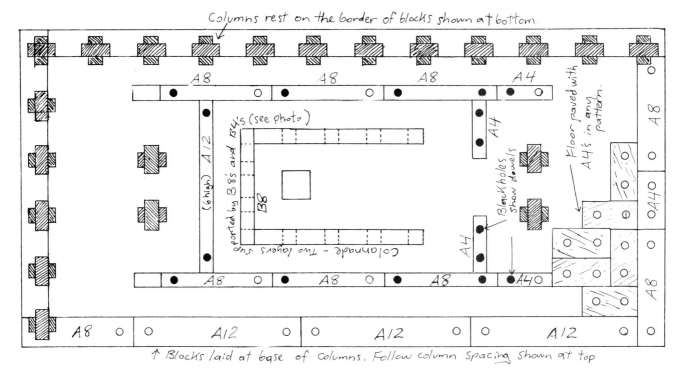

Columns rest on the border of blocks shown at bottom.

↑ Blocks laid at base of Columns. Follow column spacing shown at top

Illus. 4.10 Plan of floor and columns

Instructions

1. Lay out the floor as shown in Illus. 4.10. It is 46 block units long and 22 block units wide. Pave the whole thing with A4's according to your own idea of the "perfect" pattern. All real Greek temples also had three steps leading up to them from the outside. You can't build three steps to scale with blocks, but a row of blocks ½ block unit thick around the floor makes two steps.

2. Build 36 columns as shown in Illus. 4.8. The standard Block Set does not have quite enough A10's to go around, so you will have to substitute a combination of other blocks to do it.

3. Arrange the columns around the edge of the floor. This is called the "peristyle." It gets you right into the problems of spacing and numbers that bedeviled Greek architects. Note that there are six columns across the ends and 12 along the sides (Illus. 4.10), but the sides are *not* exactly twice the ends in length. Also, though you might expect the spaces between the columns to be exactly two block units wide like the columns themselves, that can't happen because the whole row sits back from the edge a little bit. That also means the columns don't line up exactly along the cracks in the floor paving.

4. Using rubber bands, attach the double row of blocks along the top of the columns as shown in Illus. 4.8. Illus. 4.8 and 4.9 show how these are arranged to overlap at the ends. The Greeks generally decorated the uppermost of these two rows with pictures that ran all the way around the building and, like a comic strip, told a story.

5. Build the walls inside the columns according to the plan in Illus. 4.11. Because they do not overlap at the ends, they will tend to fall over. Note that in Illus. 4.12 small blocks resting on the corners at the top prevent this.

6. Build the two-level colonnade that surrounds the statue of the god (Illus. 4.10). Use B8's for the bottom row. Use two B12's and a B8 on top of that. Then put an upper

row of B4's on top of that. The Greeks used two rows because they had to have thin columns to fit the space, but thin columns reaching all the way to the ceiling looked too skinny.

7. Make a roof out of a piece of cardboard 36″ long and 18″ wide, folded down the middle. The Greeks built roofs of tile or marble slabs. You can get the exact look of tile by using the corrugated paper that school supply shops sell in rolls for decorating bulletin boards. A pin at each corner keeps it from sliding off (Illus. 4.7).

A2	A4	A8	A8	A8	
A4		A8	A8	A8	A2
					A2

Illus. 4.11   The temple walls are built like this and pinned with dowels (dashed lines).

Illus. 4.12   Interior of Greek temple

Illus. 4.13   Todaiji Temple in Nara, Japan

Oriental Palace

Not too long after the Greeks perfected their temples, a style of building appeared in China that shows how different people can take the same idea and develop it in entirely different ways. Both the Chinese and the Greeks started from similar rectangular houses supported by wooden columns and roofed with tile, but their later buildings don't look alike at all.

The Chinese did not build their temples of stone as the Greeks did, though they used stone in walls and fortifications. They constructed their temples and palaces of wood, putting real art into their wooden roofs and beams. The same was true of Japan, and both countries produced extraordinary carpenters.

The earliest Chinese builders did not make triangular roof trusses. They only used posts with a beam across the top. To make a sloping roof, they put a shorter post-and-beam combination on top of the ceiling beams, and then an even shorter post and beam above that in a series of steps, as you can see in Illus. 4.20.

As buildings got bigger, however, the huge number of columns needed to support the roof got in the way. So, in order to make each column hold up more ceiling without having to use very long and heavy timbers, the Chinese devised a system of short branching beams. A short bracket on top of each column would hold up two more short brackets, and those would in turn hold up two more, and so on (Illus. 4.20).

This produced a dizzying number of little beams and joints even in its simplest form, but that only challenged the more able carpenters to make yet more complicated designs. Anyone who has looked at one of those intricately fitted Chinese wooden puzzles has some idea of the kind of thing these traditional architects admired. Some of their roof designs far outdo the most complicated puzzle you can buy. Then, of course, all that exposed wood just begged to be carved into

Illus. 4.14   Finished oriental palace

dragons and serpents, which the Chinese painted and gilded in extravagant ways.

The block version here is a good deal simpler and slightly different in design than the traditional Chinese or Japanese roof, but it catches the spirit pretty well. The Oriental architects were able to add extra curves and flourishes to the tops of the roofs of their buildings as well as to the supports. Unfortunately, you will have to fall back on bending cardboard for that.

Materials

Columns:
    32 A12's
    16 Short dowels

Tops of 8 Central Columns:
     8 A10's
     8 A8's
     8 A4's
     6 B8's

Tops of 8 Outside Columns:
     8 A8's
    32 C12's
    16 C10's
    16 C8's
     6 B8's

Beam Assemblies:
     8 A8's
    24 A4's
     4 B12's
     4 Short dowels

Instructions

1. The block palace in the photos was built on a mirror, but there are enough blocks in a standard Block Set to pave a platform as was done in the Greek temple project. It would be 38 block units wide and 47 long. If you wish to do that, first build all the parts described in the steps that follow and then set them to one side so that you won't

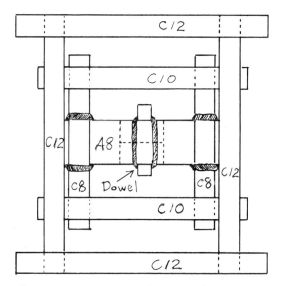

Illus. 4.15   Top view of outer column

Illus. 4.16   Side view of outer column

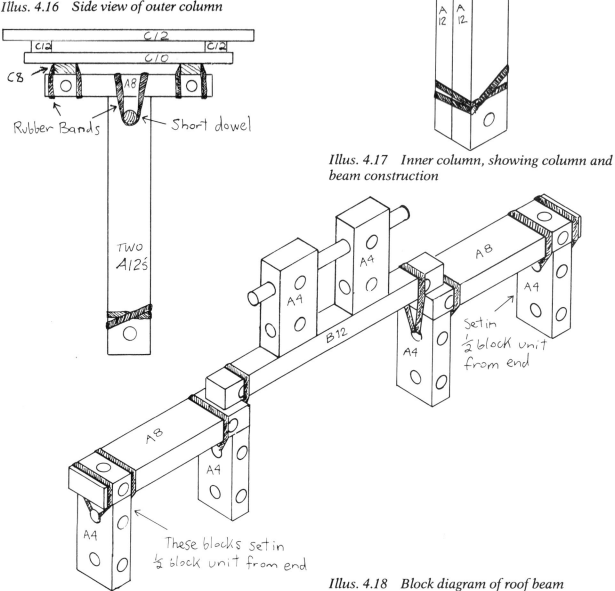

Illus. 4.17   Inner column, showing column and beam construction

Illus. 4.18   Block diagram of roof beam

Illus. 4.19   Columns and roof beams in place

use up sizes in the floor platform that you need for the rest of the structure.

2. Construct eight columns as shown in Illus. 4.17. These are the central columns. They go in two rows as shown in Illus. 4.19 and 4.20. The columns in each row stand 13 block units apart. The rows are nine block units apart.

3. Use rubber bands and B8's to connect the beams atop each central column along both rows.

4. Build eight outer columns as shown in Illus. 4.15 and 4.16. These go in two rows, one on each side of the central columns. They stand ten block units from the central rows and 13 block units from each other (Illus. 4.20 and 4.21).

5. Connect these along the outside edge by laying two B8's across neighboring brackets as seen in Illus. 4.21. Even without rubber bands these add stability and help balance the columns for the next step.

6. Build four roof-beam assemblies according to Illus. 4.18. The lower section, held together by rubber bands, can be lifted into place as one piece. Then, add the pair of A4's connected by a dowel to the top. Illus. 4.20 and 4.21 show how the columns plus beams look from front and side, as does Illus. 4.19. In that photo the outside A4's

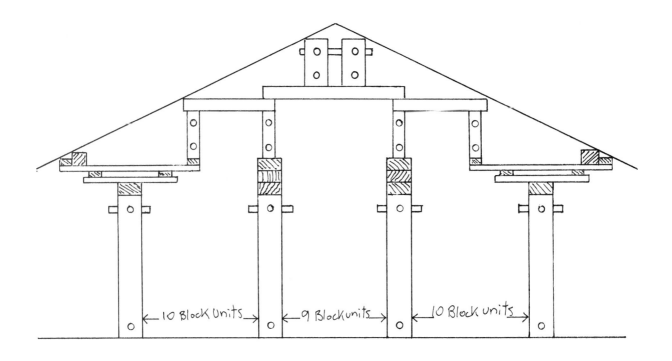

Illus. 4.20   Spacing of columns with roof beams in place (end view)

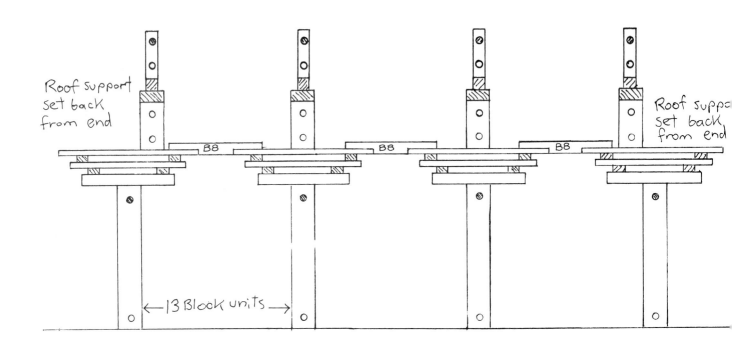

Illus. 4.21   Spacing of columns with roof beams in place (side view)

Illus. 4.22   (Opposite page) Detail of columns, beams, and steps

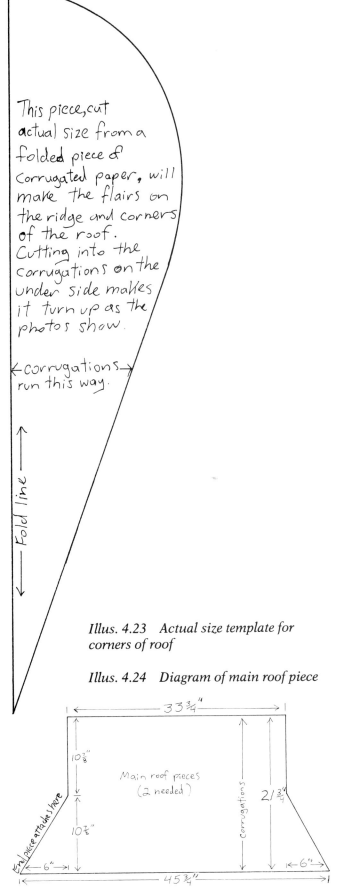

This piece, cut actual size from a folded piece of corrugated paper, will make the flairs on the ridge and corners of the roof.
Cutting into the corrugations on the under side makes it turn up as the photos show.

←corrugations→ run this way.

↑ Fold line ↓

Illus. 4.23   Actual size template for corners of roof

Illus. 4.24   Diagram of main roof piece

33¾"

10⅞"

Main roof pieces (2 needed)

Corrugations

2/3¾"

10⅞"

End piece attaches here

6"

6"

45¾"

are attached by rubber bands to the inside C12's on the supporting brackets. This is done before lifting the roof assembly into place and adds stability, but it is not absolutely necessary if you are careful on the next step.

7. Cut the roof from cardboard according to the patterns in Illus. 4.23, 4.24, and 4.25. The two end pieces connect the jutting-out ends of the main roof pieces, leaving a triangle of open space above them. Assemble the pieces with tape on the underside, and lower into place. The ideal material, which looks exactly like a tile roof, is the corrugated paper sold by the roll in school supply shops for decorating bulletin boards. One side is corrugated, the other flat. If you use this material, cut the flaring corner pieces (Illus. 4.23) from the pattern as shown, with the corrugations running crosswise. Then, slice the backing paper with a razor along all the corrugations, allowing them to be flattened out a bit. This will let them be curled up as in Illus. 4.14.

8. Use the remaining blocks to build a wall around the building as shown in Illus. 4.22, steps, or whatever decorations you wish. This basic form of building was almost always entered from the long side, so steps would be placed as in Illus. 4.14.

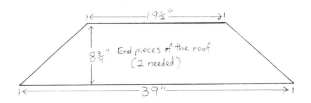

19½"

8¾"   End pieces of the roof (2 needed)

39"

Illus. 4.25   Diagram of end piece of roof

Illus. 4.26   Stonehenge

Stonehenge

At the same time that the Egyptians began cutting stones for their first pyramid, about 2800 B.C., some mysterious people in Britain began a building enterprise that would become nearly as famous.

Stonehenge is a collection of standing stones arranged in concentric circles on Salisbury Plain in southern England. The stones offer no shelter. Some of the smaller ones could only have come from 300 miles away, transported with great effort since they each weigh tons.

The stonework, though not as slick as the masonry of the Greeks, Minoans, and Egyptians, shows that the Stonehenge people could do whatever they thought important every bit as well. The outer circle of big stones, called the "Sarsen Circle," is 97½ feet across, and yet the inside faces of the uprights have been smoothed to the exact curve of that circle.

The design came from the rising and setting of the sun and moon. On the longest day of the year, June 21, a priest of the unknown people that built Stonehenge could stand in the center of the circle facing out towards a certain stone, and know that the sun would rise exactly over it. Standing at other points and looking over other markers he could also predict where the moon would rise and set, and from that perhaps foretell eclipses.

The mathematics of that are complicated to explain and more complicated still to carry out, but of course the designers of Stonehenge wasted no time on algebra and geometry. They simply watched the sky morning after morning, night after night, noting with markers on the ground where sun and moon rose and set against the distant horizon, until a pattern developed. Working in that way you could find all the astronomical relationships that were built into Stonehenge in about 19 years.

If you can build your block Stonehenge on a flat board or table on a porch or deck where the rising sun strikes, you can get some idea of how the original Stonehenge fitted into the changing of the seasons. From December 21 to

Illus. 4.27 Finished Stonehenge project

June 21 the sun rises a little farther north than it did the day before. After that, sunrise moves gradually to the south again. It's a good challenge of your ability in Stone Age astronomy to record this movement for a few days and try to predict where the sun will rise in a week or two, and then build the model to catch the first beam on that day.

If you have a clear, level horizon to the east, as you would overlooking a lake or plain, you can see the sun rising precisely due east on the first day of spring (March 21), and the first day of autumn (September 21). If you use a magnetic compass to align your model, be sure to correct for the declination in your area.

The block project layout is fairly close to scale. The fun part of building it comes from trying to figure out how the original surveyors laid it out. A 21½"-long string with a pencil tied to one end will help draw a perfect Sarsen circle 21½" in radius. No doubt the ancient builders used a rope tied to a stake in the center in much the same way. However, dividing that circle into 30 equal parts for po-

sitioning the uprights is quite a trick. A protractor makes it easier, but such things did not exist 4,500 years ago in Britain.

Materials

Outer Circle (Sarsen Circle):
   30 A8's
   22 B8's

Inner "Horse Shoe" (Trilithons):
   20 A12's
    5 A8's

Altar Stone:
   1 A4

Standing Stones:
   Assorted B4's and B2's
String
Protractor

Instructions

1. On a piece of paper draw a full circle using an ordinary protractor. Mark the center point and divide the circle into 30 12° segments.

2. Tape or tack the paper to the surface where you mean to build and draw a circle 21½"

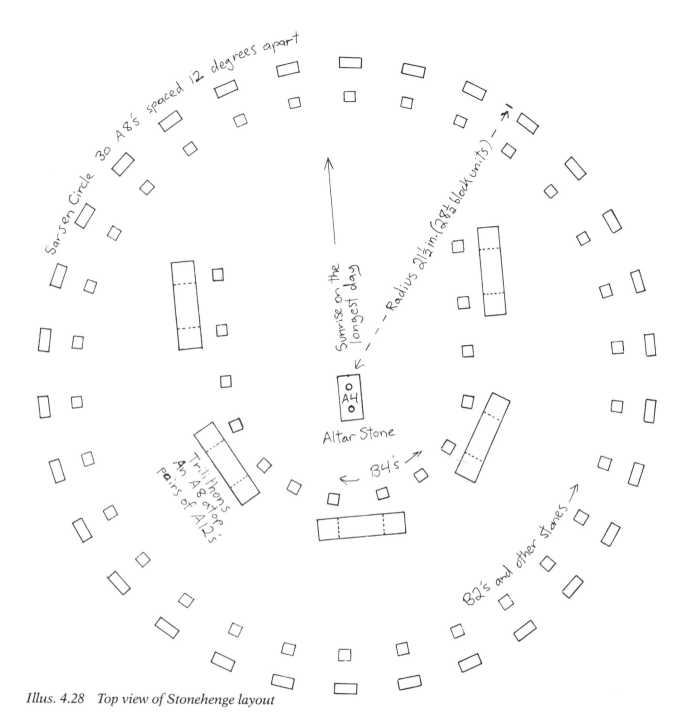

Illus. 4.28   Top view of Stonehenge layout

(28½ block units) in radius by tacking a string to the center of the protractor circle, tying on a pencil at the 21½" point, and drawing the circle with the string stretched taut.

3. Still using the pencil at the end of the string, mark the outer circle at each of the 30 places where the string crosses one of the 12° marks on the protractor circle.

4. Set up the "Sarsen Circle" of A8's on these marks and cap with B8's.

5. Pick the sunrise direction you wish to celebrate and build the horseshoe of "trilithons" to open that way and put the altar stone in the middle.

6. The rings of small stones inside the Sarsen Circle in the real Stonehenge are odd sizes, so various B2's and B4's will work here. The ring inside the trilithons should be B4's.

7. Outside the circle, place a single standing B12 to cast a shadow towards the altar.

Illus. 4.29   Harlech Castle in Wales withstood a seven-year siege.

Harlech Castle

Harlech Castle on the coast of Wales was built by Edward I of England shortly after he conquered the Welsh in 1283. It is one of a series of castles he constructed to keep his rebellious new subjects in line and it probably saw more sieges and warfare than any castle in the British Isles.

In 1404, Owen Glendower, a descendant of the last Welsh prince, rebelled and drove the English out for four years, but the English soldiers in Harlech held out against him longer than any other castle. He laid siege to it for months until all but 21 defenders starved to death. Then he made it his headquarters. When the English came back, Glendower and his men were off fighting in the mountains, but his wife, family, and son-in-law whom he hoped to make king of England were caught inside Harlech with a small guard of men. They held out for nearly a year until the son-in-law died. The English took the rest of Glendower's family captive to London, but his wife, son, and two youngest daughters died within weeks.

Fifty years later, yet another Welshman organized resistance to the English king and held Harlech for several years of siege before he also was starved out. Only starvation could

Illus. 4.30   Finished project

overcome Harlech because the design was so strong that a handful of defenders could beat off direct attacks. Castle builders all over Europe copied many of the ideas that made it so successful.

Earlier castle builders usually put up one strong tower called a "donjon," or "keep," surrounded by a wall and perhaps a moat. The strength of the tower, however, often did not help in defending the wall. If attackers got through the wall, they could easily break into the tower or starve out its defenders.

Castles like Harlech, however, had walls within walls built close together, so archers on the high walls of the "inner ward" could help defend the lower walls beyond. They also put towers right on the main wall itself. These project beyond the wall, so that archers in them could catch anyone approaching the castle in a crossfire.

The strongest towers were placed right over the weakest point in the wall, the gate. Anyone attacking that would have to break through three heavy doors, smash three iron-shod portcullises, and brave boiling oil and arrows delivered through "murder holes" in the walls and ceiling. If an enemy did get to the inner ward, he would still have to capture the towers one by one while dodging arrows from all of them.

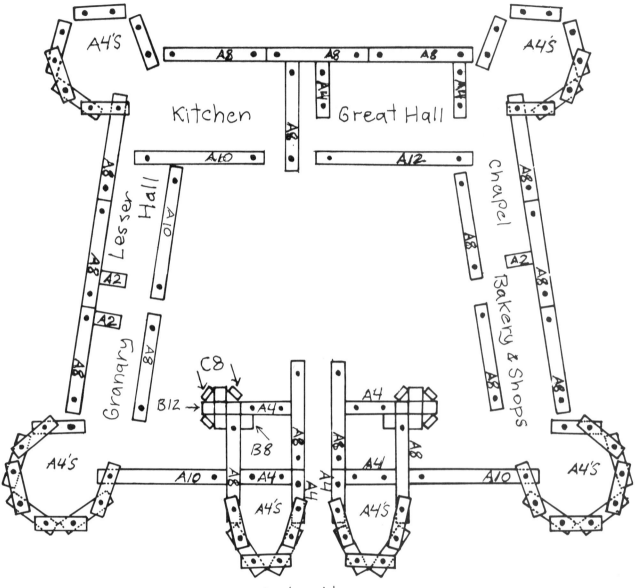

Kitchen

Great Hall

Lesser Hall

Granary

Chapel

Bakery & Shops

Gate House

Illus. 4.31 Block diagram of foundation for inner ward

Illus. 4.32 Ground plan of Harlech Castle

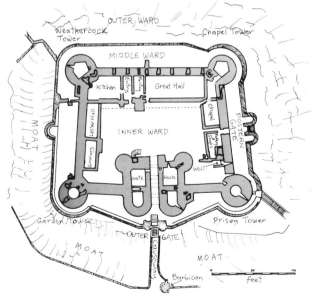

OUTER WARD

Weathercock Tower

Chapel Tower

MIDDLE WARD

Kitchen

Great Hall

MOAT

Lesser Hall

Granary

INNER WARD

Chapel

POSTERN GATE

Well

Gate House

Garden Tower

OUTER GATE

Prison Tower

MOAT

MOAT

Barbican

feet

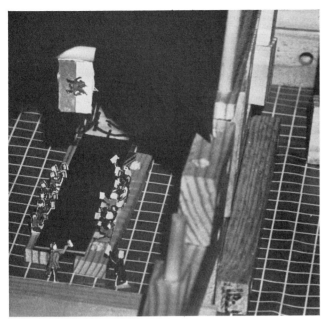

Illus. 4.33   Detail of dining hall with paper miniatures

Note that this project requires half again as much dowel length as the basic set's 14½-foot total. Long dowels are not required, as in all cases where walls are pinned together, combinations of short ones work very well, but it does create a nice effect when the ends protrude equally from the tops of the towers. The best strategy is to buy half a dozen 3-foot lengths from a hardware supplier and cut them as needed.

Materials

Front Walls:
    4 A12's
    4 A10's
    2 C12's

Side Walls:
    24 A8's
    6 C8's

Back Wall:
    12 A8's
    2 A4's
    2 C8's
    1 C12

Gatehouse Front Part of Towers:
    26 A4's

Gatehouse Back Wall:
    3 A12's
    6 A4's
    2 A2's

Gatehouse Side Walls:
    6 A8's
    6 A4's
    2 B2's

Gatehouse Covered Passage:
    2 A8's
    4 A4's
    1 B4

Front Wall over Gate:
    1 A4
    1 A8

Gatehouse Steps in Courtyard:
    1 A2
    2 B2's

Gatehouse Turrets on Back Corners:
    10 B12's
    10 B4's
    12 C8's
    2 B8's

Corner Towers:
    84 A4's

Back Corner Tower Turrets:
    2 B4's
    8 Short dowels

Interior Buildings:
    1 A12
    2 A10's
    7 A8's
    9 A4's
    6 A2's
    3 B4's
    5 B2's
    1 C12
    2 C10's
    3 C8's

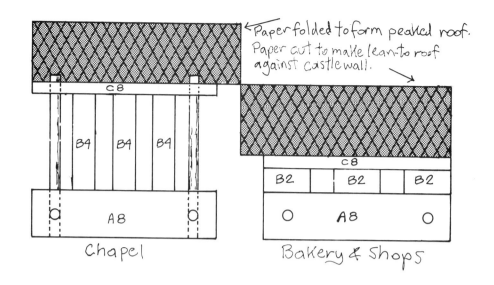

Paper folded to form peaked roof.
Paper cut to make lean-to roof
against castle wall.

Chapel

Bakery & Shops

Lean-to roof against castle wall

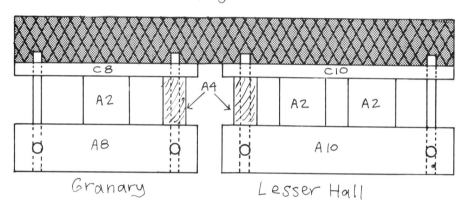

Granary

Lesser Hall

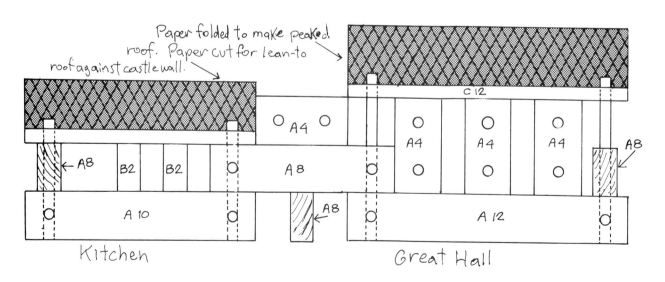

Paper folded to make peaked
roof. Paper cut for lean-to
roof against castle wall.

Kitchen

Great Hall

Illus. 4.34   Block diagram of walls to interior rooms

Illus. 4.35 Foundation of inner ward, built up a layer or two

Illus. 4.36 Detail of gate house, built up by three layers. Note paper circles for floors in corner tower.

Instructions

1. Harlech Castle stands on a rock high above the sea. It took a thousand men and horses several years to cut the stone and build it. To make a Block Set castle in a similar position, cut the approximate shape of the "middle ward" (the low wall around the main castle) out of plywood or several sheets of cardboard, put that on a box or a low stool, and cover it all with a blanket to give the effect of a high promontory. The measurements need not be exact. Simply lay out the outline of the main structure in blocks according to Illus. 4.31 and cut the general pattern freehand a few inches larger.

2. To create the effect of flagstone paving in the inner courtyard, you can use Contact shelf paper, available at any hardware dealer's.

3. Lay out the walls, towers, and gatehouse according to the plan in Illus. 4.31. Note particularly how the ends of the walls fit against the blocks of the towers.

4. Using Illus. 4.35 and 4.36 as guides for a second layer of blocks, note that
   - in the second layer, the walls between the gatehouse and the towers are A12's.
   - the back wall has an A4 in the second layer.
   - the turrets at the back corners of the gatehouse are held on by a rubber band that goes all the way around a B8 inside the corner, two dowels in the adjoining walls, and the blocks of the turret itself.

5. Start building the turrets at the back corners of the gatehouse at this point and add to them as the walls of the gatehouse rise.
   - In addition to the B8 inside the corner, the turrets are made from clusters of five B blocks rounded out with C blocks in the gaps. Study all the illustrations to see them in various stages of completion.
   - The bottom round of turret construction is a B4 in the middle, with a B12 on each side, and three C8's in the gaps.
   - The top round is a B12 in the middle surrounded by B4's on all sides and three more C8's in the gaps.
   - Use rubber bands around the corner dowels to hold them in place as you build.

6. Cut 16 cardboard circles 2 5/16" in radius to make floors for the four corner towers and give them the proper shape. This is enough for two stories, a ceiling, and a conical roof for each tower. Illus. 4.35, 4.36 and 4.38 show how they fit.

7. Repeat the layering of blocks to complete the main structure.
   - The walls have four layers, the corner towers five, and the gatehouse six.
   - Cardboard cutouts will make good floors for the gatehouse, if you want to make realistic apartments, murder holes, etc.
   - Note that in the top layer of the walls, blocks are laid sideways to form the wide "wall walk" and the overhanging parapet, seen clearly on the left-hand wall in Illus. 4.38. Rows of C8's and C12's stood on edge and set around the wall walks make battlements to protect the defenders. In fact, the real Harlech Castle did not have overhanging stone parapets, but in time of siege wooden ones called "hoardings" were built so that rocks, arrows, and hot tar could be poured straight down on attackers.

8. Lay out the floor plan of the interior buildings (Great Hall, etc.) according to Illus. 4.31. Then build up the walls according to the plans in Illus. 4.34. Cardboard or paper makes good roofing that can be lifted off to show what's going on inside.

9. Add the turrets on the two back towers. Illus. 4.38 shows these made of B4's rounded out with short dowels held on by rubber bands.

10. Add banners on matchstick poles and whatever paper figures you wish. The scale is about 5/32" = 1 foot, so a man done as a cutout would stand about 7/8" high.

Illus. 4.37   (Top) Detail of gatehouse and drawbridge

Illus. 4.38   (Bottom) Alternate view of finished project

Illus. 4.39 Neuschwanstein Castle, built by Ludwig II of Bavaria, is the most photographed fairy castle of all.

Fairy Castle

Fairy castles are like fairy tales. They have gotten better in the telling. A hut became a strong house. Then the house sprouted a tower, and if one tower, then why not half a dozen, and why should the tallest not rise into the clouds? And why shouldn't the dungeon be blacker and deeper than a coal mine? And why shouldn't the throne room glow from a million candles in crystal chandeliers? After all, a marble ballroom costs a storyteller nothing.

Just as many people today would like to live like TV stars, so some princes and princesses of old often tried to make their lives as much like fairy tales as possible, and so they built their own fairy castles in stone. The

Illus. 4.40   Finished fairy castle

"Mad Duke," Ludwig II of Bavaria, who spent a good deal of his youth building castles in the air, undertook to build them in stone as soon as he got his hands on the key to the Bavarian treasury. He built several fantastic palaces, all in different styles.

A few castles really had maidens imprisoned in their towers and ogres (or at least very evil men) in their dungeons. Some had very grand ballrooms where princes and princesses danced in finery as fancy as anything Cinderella's Fairy Godmother ever created.

The block castle here tries to show something of how fairy castles grew. Like many of those in Germany and Central Europe, it starts from just a big house. The towers are added on, and each one is different. Tall towers did in fact have a military purpose. An arrow or a stone shot *down* from one strikes a lot harder than the same arrow shot up from below. The turret at the top stuck out over the wall so that defenders could drop rocks and boiling oil straight down on anyone below. Steep roofs shingled with slate rock kept fire arrows from doing any damage. On the other hand, many towers were built taller and pointier than necessary, just for style.

The block castle may be decorated in any way you wish. The double spiral staircase, however, comes from the Chateau of Chambord, and was designed for the French King Francis I in 1519 by the Italian architect, engineer, inventor, and artist Leonardo da Vinci. Leonardo had an extraordinary imagination that invented many contraptions, including parachutes, long before their time. He liked to design things that weren't quite what they seemed. His staircase looks like a regular spiral, but its two flights never cross. One can imagine two swordsmen duelling round and round each other without ever meeting.

This project requires a large number of dowels, totalling 46 feet, which is a bit more than half again as many as recommended for an initial supply for the Block Set. The spiral stairs and the roof trusses require specific lengths. For pinning together the walls a variety of combinations of smaller dowels will work as long as they come out evenly at the top of the wall. If you haven't already accumulated an additional complement of dowels, the best strategy is to buy half a dozen 3-foot lengths from the hardware dealer and cut them as necessary.

You will also need six sheets of poster board to make the floors, roofs, and inside supports of the round towers. A hand-held hole puncher is also helpful in making holes for the dowels in the poster board.

Materials

Front Towers:
    99 A4's

Front Wall:
    3 A12's
    3 A10's
    6 A8's
    4 A4's
    2 A2's
    2 B2's

Right Wall:
    3 A12's
    11 A10's
    5 A8's
    3 A4's
    1 A2
    1 B2

Left Wall:
    3 A12's
    4 A10's
    2 A4's
    1 B2

Front and Side Walls of Square Tower:
    20 A8's

Short Round Tower:
    10 C12's
    10 C10's
    5 B4's
    5 B2's
    3 Wheels
    Cardboard

Tall Round Tower:
    10 C12's
    10 C10's
    10 C8's

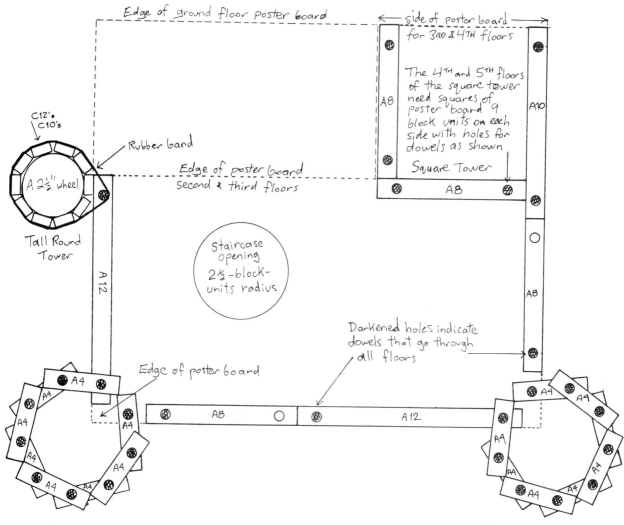

Edge of ground floor poster board

side of poster board
for 3RD & 4TH floors

The 4TH and 5TH floors
of the square tower
need squares of
poster board 9
block units on each
side with holes for
dowels as shown

Square Tower

A8   A10

A8

C12's
C10's

Rubber band

Edge of poster board
second & third floors

A 2½" wheel

Tall Round
Tower

A12

staircase
opening
2½-block-
units radius

A8

Darkened holes indicate
dowels that go through
all floors

Edge of poster board

A4   A4
A4   A4
A4   A4
A4   A4
A4   A4

A8   A12

A4   A4
A4   A4
A4   A4
A4   A4
A4   A4

Illus. 4.41   Block diagram of fairy castle

5 B4's
5 B2's
4 Wheels

Roof Trusses:
    8 C12's
    9 C8's
    6 Dowels 18 block units long

Spiral Stairs:
    8 A8's
    12 C8's
    7 Dowels 11 block units long

Front Entrance:
    1 A10
    7 A8's
    2 B8's
    2 B4's
    2 B2's
    3 C10's
    Poster board for floors and roofs

Illus. 4.42   A view of the spiral staircase from above

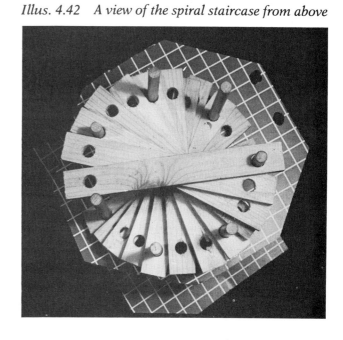

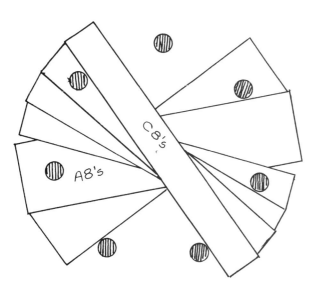

Illus. 4.43   *The stairs are built on seven dowels. The lower level of A8's is hitched to a dowel at one end only. The upper level uses C8's and every other one is not hitched at all.*

Illus. 4.44   *The spiral staircase*

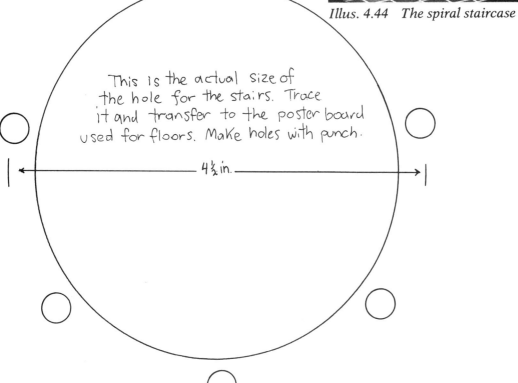

This is the actual size of the hole for the stairs. Trace it and transfer to the poster board used for floors. Make holes with punch.

← 4½ in. →

Illus. 4.45   *Template for stairway hole through floor*

Instructions

1. Outline the ground plan (without the small round tower) on top of a piece of poster board according to Illus. 4.41. Use a carpenter's square or other true right angle to get the corners as precise as possible. Notice particularly the position of the blocks of the front wall in relation to the corners of the poster board.

2. Draw around the outside of the blocks to get the exact size of the ground-floor rectangle, and also the side of the square tower and back edge of the upper stories, which are shown by a dotted line in Illus. 4.41.

3. Before you move the blocks, also mark the position of dowel holes on the cardboard by putting a pencil right down through the blocks at all the places marked by darkened holes in Illus. 4.41, which show where dowels must pass through.

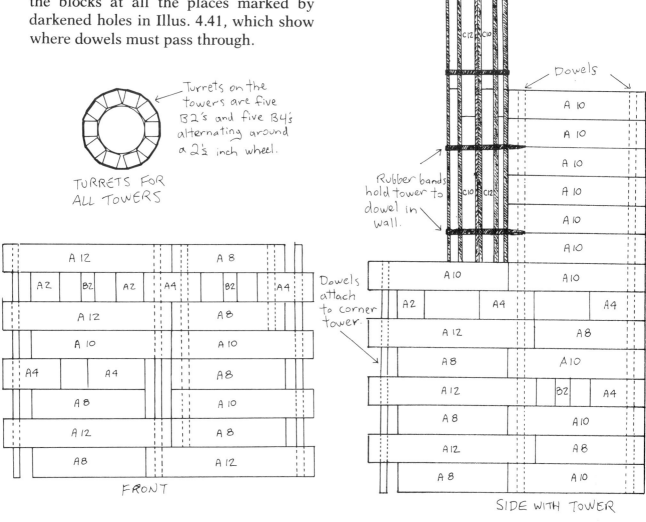

Dowels attach to levels of towers on the corners.

SIDE

Turrets on the towers are five B2's and five B4's alternating around a 2½ inch wheel.

TURRETS FOR ALL TOWERS

Dowels

Rubber bands hold tower to dowel in wall.

Dowels attach to corner tower.

FRONT

SIDE WITH TOWER

Illus. 4.46   Block diagrams of walls and turrets, with notes on attaching towers to walls

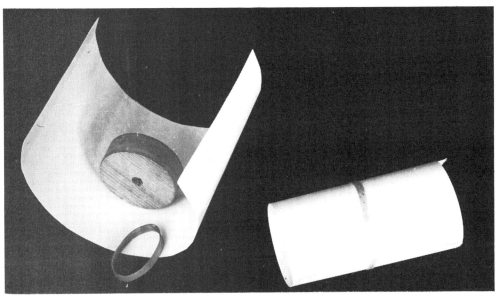

Illus. 4.47   Use wheel and poster board to construct the tower.

Illus. 4.48   The poster board rolls are surrounded by C blocks.

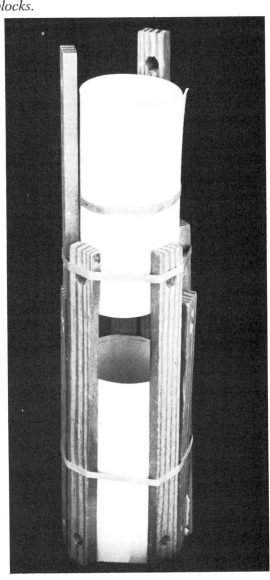

4. Cut out the rectangular shape of the ground floor. Cut two more floors to the L shape of the actual building. They stop short at the dotted line in Illus. 4.41 and extend into the square tower. None of the floor pieces extends into the round

5. Stack up the floor pieces and punch the dowel holes according to the marks made on the original tracing. Punch several times to make holes big enough to allow a dowel to pass through without friction.

6. The staircase passes through both upper floors. Trace the circle and dowel holes shown in Illus. 4.45 on one of the poster-board cutouts in the approximate position shown in the ground plan. (This is easier if you make a photocopy of Illus. 4.45 that you can put right on the poster board.) Cut out the circle and then line up the two floor pieces and cut the same circle in the second one. Holding both together, punch the seven dowel holes through both sheets with a paper punch.

7. Building on top of the ground floor poster board, put up two layers of blocks, including the corner towers. Illus. 4.46 shows which blocks to use in each of the three main walls (the castle is open in back) and where to put the dowels. Pay particular

Illus. 4.49 (Below) Block diagram of tall round tower

Illus. 4.50 (Right) Completed short round tower and tall round tower

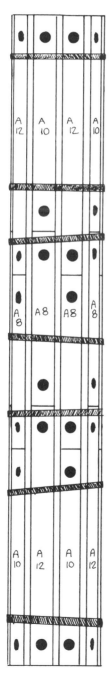

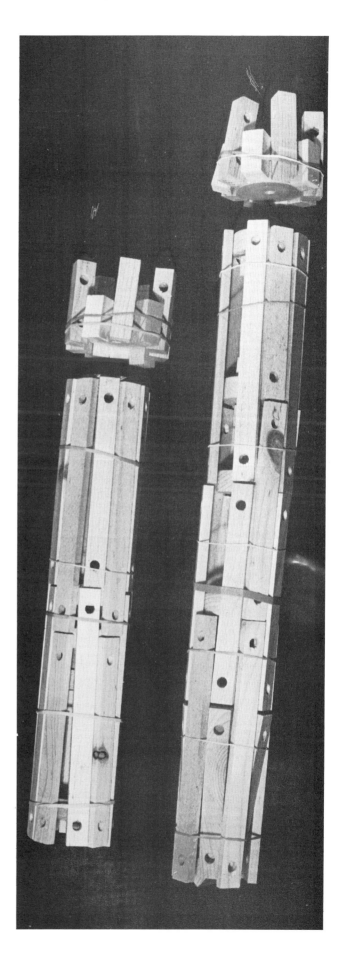

Illus. 4.51   The three roof trusses

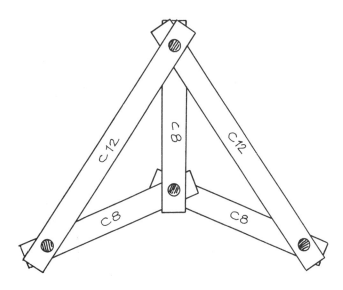

Illus. 4.52   Block diagram of roof truss

Illus. 4.53   (Opposite page) The fairy castle as seen from the back. Note that the square tower has an extra two floors. The back of the project stays open, like a doll's house.

attention to getting the round corner towers started right.

8. Fit the second floor poster board, containing the staircase hole, down over the dowels sticking up from the walls.

9. Using four A8's, build the spiral staircase up to the second floor level as shown in Illus. 4.43 and 4.44. Push dowels down from the top to hold them in place. Note that each block has a dowel only through one end.

10. Using 12 C8's and three more dowels, build up the rest of the staircase as shown in Illus. 4.42, 4.43, and 4.44. Note that every other step does not hitch to a dowel at all. The others hitch only at one end.

11. Start building the bottom section of the tall round tower at the back left corner. The whole tower requires three paper rolls made by rolling a piece of poster board around a wheel as shown in Illus. 4.47. Surround the first roll with alternating C12's and C10's as shown in Illus. 4.48 and 4.49.

12. Attach this first section of the tower to the corner with a rubber band over the dowel as shown in Illus. 4.41.

13. Build the walls up three more levels of blocks, and then put in the poster-board floor as before. Then build another three levels. At each level, add to the round tower at the back left corner and secure it to the corner dowel with rubber bands.

14. As a convenient but optional feature you can cut another rectangle of poster board to make a deck extending from the square tower across to the front wall. This will also create a balcony inside the great hall at the top of the stairs.

15. The big square tower has six more levels above the wall level. It also needs two additional poster-board floor pieces (see Illus. 4.41 and 4.53). These should be 9 block units square, with holes punched for dowels as shown in Illus. 4.42. Install the first at the height of the main walls (and the deck if you put one in) and the second, three layers up. As you build, start the short round tower at the same

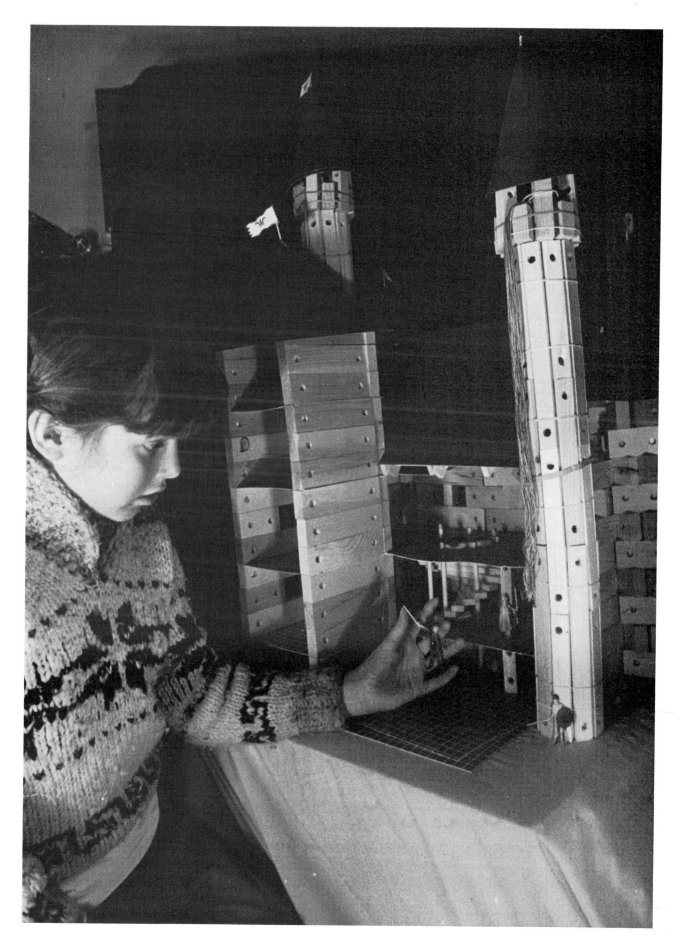

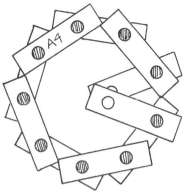

Illus. 4.54 The front corner towers turn inward once they are taller than the top of the wall.

time, and secure it to dowels in the square tower. Illus. 4.46 and 4.56 show how it fits.

16. Carry the front corner towers up as high as you wish. The photos show one of them with 11 levels of blocks and the other one with 12. Note in Illus. 4.54 and 4.56 how the levels above the top of the wall have one block turned inward to fill the place where the ends of the wall blocks would otherwise attach.

Illus. 4.55 Diagrams for paper roofs

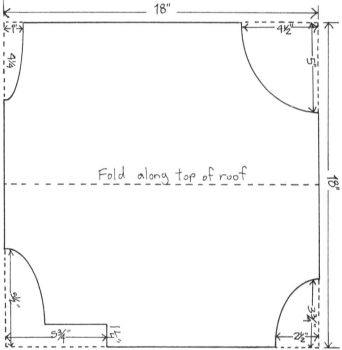

Main roof over great hall.

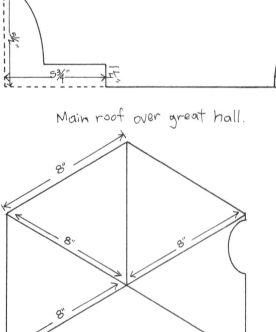

Roof for square tower

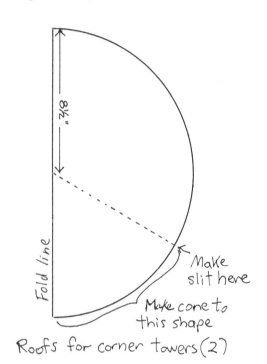

Roofs for corner towers (2)

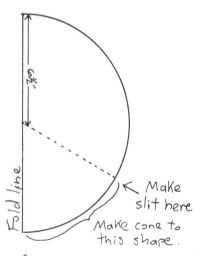

Roofs for round towers (2)

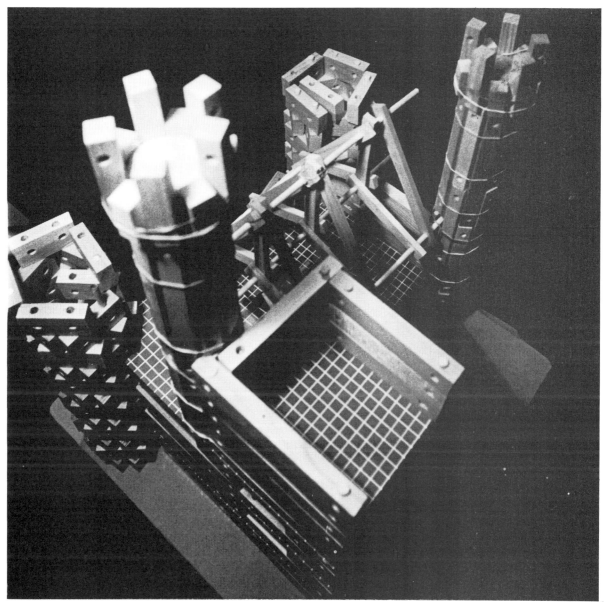

Illus. 4.56   View of project before roofs are put on

17. Assemble the three roof trusses according to Illus. 4.51 and 4.52. This will take four dowels about 18 block units long that go through all the trusses.

18. Make turrets for the small round towers by securing alternating B4's and B2's around a wheel with a rubber band (Illus. 4.46). When you set them on top of the towers, the wheel can be pushed down a little to fit inside the tower itself. Another rubber band at that point will hold the turret there.

19. Lay out and cut roof parts from poster board (Illus. 4.55). The front towers will each use half of a circle 8½" in radius. The small towers will each use half of a circle 6½" in radius. Slide one edge of these half-circles over the other until you get the right steepness; then tape or glue in place. Cut the roof for the square tower, and crease the bends at the corners. Then tape the edges together from the underside. Finally, set them all in place.

20. Build an entryway or drawbridge according to your own design. Few castles had any mechanism as complicated as the Tower Bridge project earlier in this book, but with a bit of string and some imagination, you could certainly make one that will raise and lower.

Illus. 4.57 Chartres Cathedral

Chartres Cathedral

Most block builders stick to bridges, castles, houses, and toys, because churches seem a bit too serious for the living room floor. On the other hand, the most astounding block structures on Earth of any kind are the great cathedrals built in Europe in the Middle Ages. At 404 feet, the tower of Salisbury Cathedral in England stood taller than any human creation except for the Pyramids until modern times. (In 1551, the French put a 501-foot steeple atop the cathedral at Beauvais, but it fell a few years later.)

The people who built these incredible buildings had no steel beams, cables, power winches or cement. They had only stone blocks cut laboriously by hand and stuck together by the weakest of mortar. The architects who led the work never studied higher mathematics or engineering. Not a few of them started learning their trade as day laborers cutting stone in quarries and they simply observed, experimented, and used common sense until they could do what no one had done before. Sometimes they failed, as they did at Beauvais, where the first roof vaults fell, as well as the steeple.

No other project will make you feel so much like the actual builders of a great work as putting up this block cathedral.

Although our block church has a spire in the middle instead of two towers on the front, it is modelled after Chartres Cathedral in France, which has probably inspired more architects and engineers than any building in the last 800 years. You might build your church in still a different way, however, and still be true to the spirit of Chartres, because it is a combination of many ideas and events that happened to come together in one place.

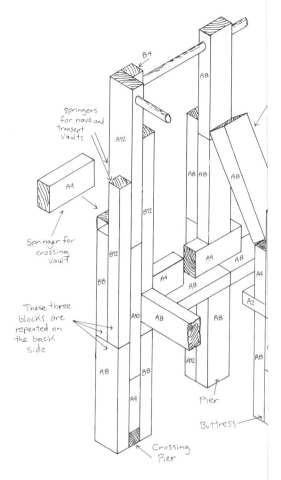

Illus. 4.61 Block diagram of buttresses an[...]

■ Outside these, stack a pair of A[...]
  flat, a pair of A4's standing on[...]
  single A4 laid flat, and a single [...]
  A4.

4. Thread dowels through the top[...]
   piers and front towers, attaching t[...]
   parts of the as-yet-unassembl[...]
   trusses as you do this. Illus. 4.6[...]
   these trusses in various stages of c[...]
   tion. If you don't have dowels long[...]
   to go the whole length of the nave[...]
   nations of dowels that meet in[...]
   tops of the piers will work.

   ■ Each truss takes one C8 and on[...]
     each side (Illus. 4.60). In Illus. [...]
     can see these hanging in pairs f[...]
     dowels above the nave. In Ill[...]
     completed trusses over one tran[...]
     the choir show how the long a[...]
     pieces on opposite sides mu[...]
     properly in the middle.

Illus. 4.58 Finished cathedral project

Illus. 4.60   The block project compared

- The row of A8's that conne[c]
  of the nave and the choir
  will help stabilize them som

- The piers at the ends of th
  have A4's laid flat at this p
  of A8's like the piers of th[e]
  standing on edge on top of t[h]
  in Illus. 4.61, connect to [t]
  piers.

- The two piers that round o
  end of the choir can wait u
  the rest of the construction
  They also have A4's laid fla[t]
  necting point, as seen in Ill[u]
  on edge connect them to ea[c]
  the other piers of the choir[.]

- The A8's that connect the
  to the first piers of the n[a]
  naturally in one of the [ ]
  towers.

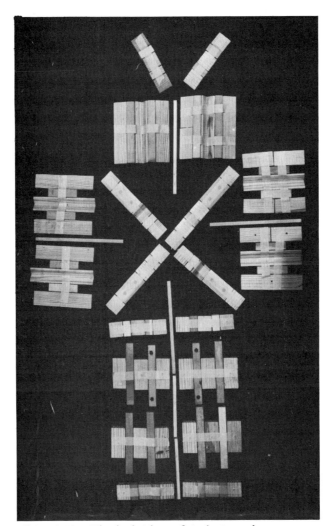

Illus. 4.63   Blocks laid out for choir and transept vaults, with crossing vaults at center

of bread through A and B, you would see the cross section shown in Illus. 4.60, except that the left half is Chartres. (Chartres had more flying buttresses to stiffen the piers against wind and the weight of the vault.)

- Illus. 4.60 and 4.62 also show the vaulted ceiling. These vaults (arches) weren't actually necessary to keep out the rain because of the roofs above. However, the medieval masons built them—as high and as wide as possible —for the sake of beauty, as an act of worship (they appear to soar heavenwards), and to show off their skill. It was difficult and very dangerous work. The stone was laid over wooden forms called "centering" and covered by 4″ of mortar. Crowds watched in terrible sus-

pense when the centering was removed, and the masons found out if their work would stand or fall. Putting up the block vaults is nearly as nerve-wracking, even without the risk of falling 120 feet onto the pavement.

7. Tape the roof vaults together as shown in Illus. 4.63 and 4.64, and lift them into place. Each pier has a step or "springer" to receive the end of a vault. Illus. 4.67 shows one in position over the choir.

- Build the choir and transept vaults first (Illus. 4.63).

- Set the taped vault halves on the springers and lean them together; then slip C blocks in as "keystones" at the top of the vaults.

- The choir and the transept vaults each take one C12 as a keystone. Start them from the outside, but don't slide them

Illus. 4.64   Blocks laid out for nave roof vault

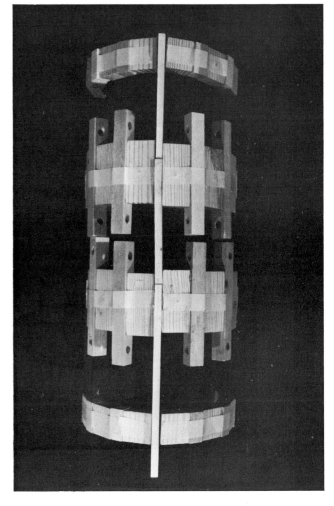

Illus. 4.65   The vaults in place

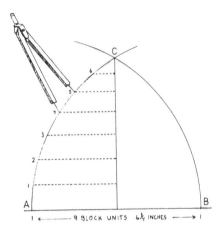

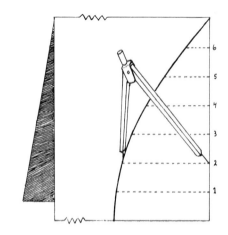

You can make a common gothic arch across A-B by putting the compass point on A and drawing B-C, then putting the point on B and drawing A-C.

To cut paper vaults that will fit perfectly where they cross, you have to measure the length of A-C along the curve. Set your compass or dividers at one inch apart and "walk" the points along the curve. Here the curve is a little over 7 steps long.

For the vault itself, fold a piece of paper as wide as the distance you just measured, and mark off the same steps with the compass along the straight edge, so the straight edge of your paper is the length of the curve of the arch.

Next you've got to cut the folded paper so it will fit exactly at the crossing of the vault. Use your compass to measure the distance from each step along the curve of your first arch to the center line. Then mark this same distance back from the edge of your folded paper at the same step. That will give you a new, steeper curve.

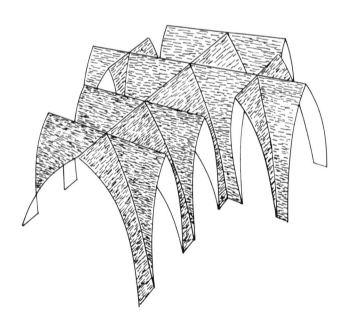

When you bend your paper to the curve of the first arch, you will find that four pieces fit together at the crossing. In a stone cathedral there are little crossings at each window. Since the window arches are narrower than the main vault, the drawings are more complicated, though the idea is the same. I'll let you figure it out.

You will have to tape these vaults to the piers, because they won't match the springers I designed for my block vaults.

Illus. 4.66   Directions for making gothic arches for roofs out of paper

Illus. 4.67   (Opposite page) Buttresses and piers set out over sketched-in ground plan. Note roof trusses in place.

all the way in or you will have no room for setting the crossing vaults.

- Set the crossing vaults on the A4 springers lower down on the crossing piers.
- Set the vaults of the nave, starting at the crossing, adding the keystone pieces as you add vaults.
- Slide the C12 keystones of transept and nave vaults all the way in so that they

nearly reach the tops of the crossing vaults.

8. Position the piers and buttresses at the end of the choir. Attach a pair of C12's as roof trusses to a short dowel through the top of each pier and pinch the loose ends together with a rubber band. Illus. 4.67 shows one of these in position, leaning against the peak of the truss over the choir.

9. Lean half-arches from the springers on these end piers against the choir vault (see Illus. 4.68), and set the flying buttresses.

10. Use leftover blocks to build a central spire, if you wish. Start by laying two A12's across the tops of the crossing piers; then continue upwards log-cabin fashion but using smaller and smaller blocks. You can instead roof over the crossing and build steeples on the front, as the Chartres builders did.

11. Cover the roof and the aisles with paper or cardboard, as in Illus. 4.67. Construction paper works well.

   ▪ The strips over the aisles are approximately 5" wide and 16" long.

   ▪ The main roof over the nave, choir, and transept is 20" wide, folded in half. The nave roof is 21" long. The transepts and choir roofs are 6".

   ▪ To make a conical piece to cover the end of the choir, cut a semicircle 10" in radius, bend it into shape and tape it to the main roof (Illus. 4.68).

   ▪ Roof pieces to cover the ambulatory are irregular in shape and best cut to fit the actual situation, as slight differences in positioning the buttresses will make a considerable difference (Illus. 4.68).

12. To show the block cathedral's scale, cut figures from paper. A 6-foot human would stand about ⅞" high (Illus. 4.65 and 4.66).

Illus. 4.68   Detail of roof pieces over ambulatory

*Illus. 4.69   An upward look at the transept:
the crossing vaults*

Illus. 4.70   A Navaho hogan

Navajo Hogan

The Navajo Indians of the American Southwest still build a traditional round or many-sided house called a hogan. For the Navajo a hogan is even more than a home: It is also a kind of church, since many ceremonies of the Navajo religion can only be performed in the hogan. That explains in part why so many Navajos who live in rectangular houses often build a hogan in the backyard. But there is another reason as well. For the high deserts of Navajo country, a hogan is almost the perfect building. The thermometer drops to 20°F below zero in winter and may rise to 110° above in summer, and at any time of year will drop 40° between noon and midnight.

A hogan's thick wooden walls and earth-covered roof store heat in the day and give it back at night, so even without a fire, it im-

proves on the outside climate greatly. And, of course, a rather small stove in the middle of a round room gives the most even heat on the least amount of fuel.

Also, in a place where long timbers are hard to find and harder still to transport, the hogan has another advantage. It requires only short logs. One can make a dome 16 feet across out of 4- or 5-foot pieces, and that without any nails or complicated joints. Navajos sometimes refer to the peculiar roof style as "whirling logs."

Some strict rules govern hogans. Being a model of the larger world, the door always faces east towards the rising sun, and no window should open to the north as that is the direction of darkness and the route taken by spirits of the dead. When moving about during a ceremony people always go clockwise around the fire because the sun moves that way through the sky. As a place of life, no one

Illus. 4.71   Finished block project hogan

should continue to live in a hogan where someone has died.

Materials

Walls:

   36 A8's
    2 A4's
    1 A2
    1 B8
    1 B4
    1 B2

Roof:

   C *blocks of various lengths*

Instructions

1. The block hogan here is built with walls of three layers of A8's pinned at the corners with dowels (Illus. 4.71). It has eight sides, though hogans may have any number.

2. The roof forms a dome. You will have to figure out the roof yourself (Illus. 4.72 and 4.73) as no Navajo builder ever had a written plan to follow.

3. The stove inside (Illus. 4.73) was cut from a small tomato paste can, and it looks very much like stoves the Navajos often make by cutting an oil drum in half.

   If you wanted to actually cover the roof with dirt as in Illus. 4.70, you would have to first fill in the gaps between the roof logs with smaller sticks, then brush, then grass. During ceremonies, you would take out the stove and build a fire right on the floor, and even if you had a regular hinged door for daily use, you would replace it with a blanket or buckskin when the medicine man came.

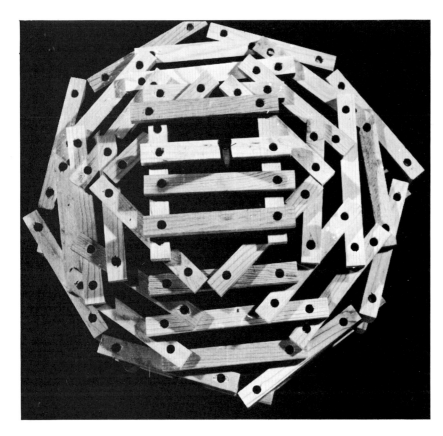

Illus. 4.72   (Above) "Whirling logs"-style roof

Illus. 4.73   (Below) Interior of block hogan

Illus. 4.74   The Astrodome in Houston, Texas

The Sports Dome

Today, we build our most extravagant buildings for business and sports. The Astrodome in Houston, Texas, was the first dome big enough to allow outdoor sports to go on inside. It was built in 1965. The dome rises 208 feet above the ground and is 642 feet in diameter. A respectable pyramid would fit under it if you took out the 52,000 seats.

For 2,500 years or more people have built domes using the principle of the arch: One piece pushes against another so that none can fall. The Astrodome has ten triangular panels (Illus. 4.74), all trying to fall into the center, but in doing so, they all crowd together and hold each other up. Following the success of the Astrodome, many similar stadiums have been built, and this block sports dome is one more variation on the theme.

Materials
Dome:
   32 A12's
   24 A10's
   24 A8's
   21 A4's
   22 *feet of dowels in varying lengths*

Risers:
   56 A4's
    8 A8's

Props for Entrance:
   2 B12's
  16 Dowels

Instructions
1. Note that, because two more A10's are called for than the set contains, you will have to substitute groups of four C10's.
2. The block dome here is built in panels like the Astrodome, though it has only eight

Illus. 4.75   The finished sports dome

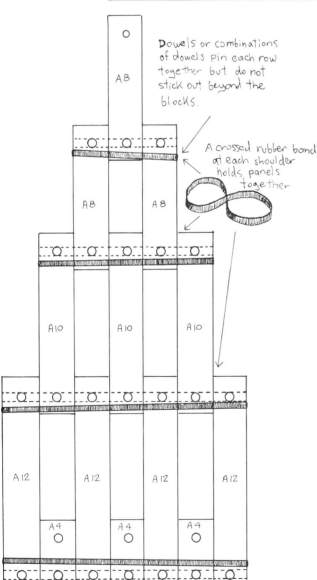

Dowels or combinations of dowels pin each row together but do not stick out beyond the blocks.

A crossed rubber band at each shoulder holds panels together

Illus. 4.76   Block diagram for one of the dome panels

panels. Make all of them according to Illus. 4.76 before assembling the dome itself.

3. Note that the dowels in the dome do not stick out beyond the sides of the rows of blocks making up the dome panels (Illus. 4.77 and 4.78). This can cause difficulties, but you do not need a single dowel for each level. Two or three shorter ones will work if they do not meet at the crack between blocks.

4. Use rubber bands twisted into a figure eight at each shoulder of the panels to join them together (Illus. 4.76). It helps to put these in advance along one side of every panel before you start putting panels together. Two or three strong ones may be necessary at each point.

5. After you have three panels firmly joined, they will lean together enough to support each other, and the rest follow easily.

6. When the whole dome is together, you can stop there, or jack it up on small piles of blocks held by dowels as shown in Illus. 4.75. Do that one or two blocks at a time, all the way around, until you reach the desired height.

Illus. 4.77   Detail of dome panels

Illus. 4.78   Another view of the finished sports dome

Skyscraper

Skyscrapers are a particularly American invention. All but two of the world's 22 tallest buildings are in the United States, and the other two are in Toronto, Canada. All but seven are in New York or Chicago. The championship has passed back and forth between these two cities several times and is currently held by the Sears Tower in Chicago, which reaches 1,559 feet at the top of its TV antenna.

All of these supertall buildings are held up by a steel frame very much like a truss bridge, an idea first applied to buildings in Chicago in 1884. The city never looked back, or down.

If you used dowels in building this block skyscraper, you could get some of the strength and flexibility that allow real skyscrapers to sway in the wind without falling, but that would get tedious and require a huge number of dowels. In any case, the standard Block Set will build a tower far higher than most indoor ceilings will allow, and knowing that it would not fall would ruin the enormous suspense that starts mounting at about the 6-foot level.

The skyscraper in the photos here at one point reached over 18 feet, only 87 times shorter than the Sears Tower, but the gentlest of breezes blew the top off. To undertake such a project, the base must be absolutely level. To build one outdoors, the engineers in Illus. 4.79 nailed a piece of heavy plywood to three stakes driven in the ground, then tapped on it with a hammer until a good mason's level showed it perfectly level.

The great moment in skyscraper building comes at the point of knocking it down. Do you throw something at it, kick it and run, or merely yank out one of the bottom blocks? (Illus. 4.81). Scientists who study the effects of earthquakes and nuclear explosions actually get paid for doing such things.

Materials

Theoretically, you could use all the blocks in the set. That would build a tower 25'2¼" tall if all the levels used two blocks. Such a structure, however, would require extraordinarily accurate blocks, an absolutely level starting surface, and no wind.

Illus. 4.79   Skyscraper in progress

Instructions

Simply stack the blocks in pairs, alternating direction in log-cabin fashion. No dowel connections are necessary, though of course they would add considerable strength.

Illus. 4.80 shows a skyscraper that has the longest blocks at the bottom and shorter ones up top, which is obviously the most stable form. But you can also put bulges in the middle, large sections on top, or whatever you wish.

Illus. 4.80   Construction continues with the smaller blocks

Illus. 4.81   The finale: an imminent crash

▪ 5 ▪
Siege Engines
and Things
that Throw

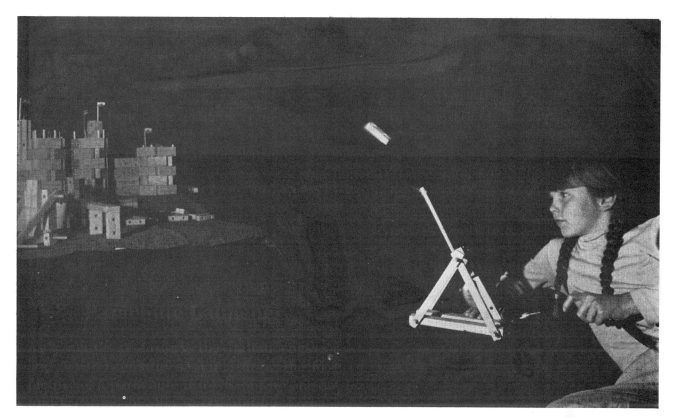

The discovery of gunpowder put an end to knights in armor and their castles. For over a thousand years before that time, however, the best defense was a high stone wall. Generations of engineers tried to find a handier weapon of siegecraft than starvation to beat that defense, and although none of their inventions ever worked as well as cannon and blasting powder, some of them came close.

In very ancient times, attackers broke into forts by digging under a wall or smashing a hole through with a battering ram. Soon someone discovered that miners didn't have to dig all the way through and fight their way out of a hole. Often they could simply undermine the wall. To hold up the ceiling of their cave while they dug, they used wooden props. Then they lit a huge fire, cleared out and waited for the wood to burn, the hole to cave in, and the wall to fall.

Battering-ram technology also changed direction. A team of men trundling a log back and forth while people above poured boiling oil on them made slow progress. Why not find a way to sling 1,000-pound rocks at the wall from a safe distance? Why not sling 1,000-pound rocks over the wall and let them smash things inside? Why not throw pots of "Greek fire" (something like napalm)? Why not shoot big spears at the people on the walls instead of measly arrows?

The machines that did these things had many names, and since very few still exist, details of the exact designs have been lost, but according to old records of what they did, they must have been quite impressive.

The trebuchet described here, when worked by a one-pound fishing sinker, threw a rather small block about ten feet. Imagine the size of a trebuchet big enough to throw half a ton or more!

Our block catapult works by rubber band, which did not exist in medieval times. Ropes made of hair (human hair worked best) did the job then. The model catapult heaves a good acorn. How many pigtails would it take to hurl a man-sized rock?

The block ballista launches matchstick and toothpick darts very well by means of a rubber band. In earlier days, it would have required a springy piece of wood of terrific strength and quality to drive a lance through the chain mail of a watchman on a high tower.

Illus. 5.1   *Finished trebuchet with iron counterweight at left, and missile at right hooked to throwing arm*

Trebuchet

The drawing and the photographs differ in some details, although the basic design is the same. Much depends on what you use for a counterweight. Fishing sinkers or the lead weights used to balance tires work perfectly, but a sock full of rocks will also do.

Materials

    3 B8's
    5 C12's
    3 Dowels
    1 Lead weight
    1 Paper clip
      Rubber bands

Instructions

1. Assemble the block trebuchet according to Illus. 5.2. The drawing shows B8's as the base of the frame, but one made with A10's in the base as shown in the photos probably won't dump over as easily.

2. Bend one loop of a paper clip around the end of the throwing arm, and the other loop into a hook. This will hook into blocks of various sizes and anything else fitted with a loop or a ring. Or, lash on the end of a plastic spoon to throw marbles, etc.

3. To launch, push down on the end of the throwing arm; then release. The heavy lead counterweight will drop, pitching up the throwing arm and hurling the missile into the air.

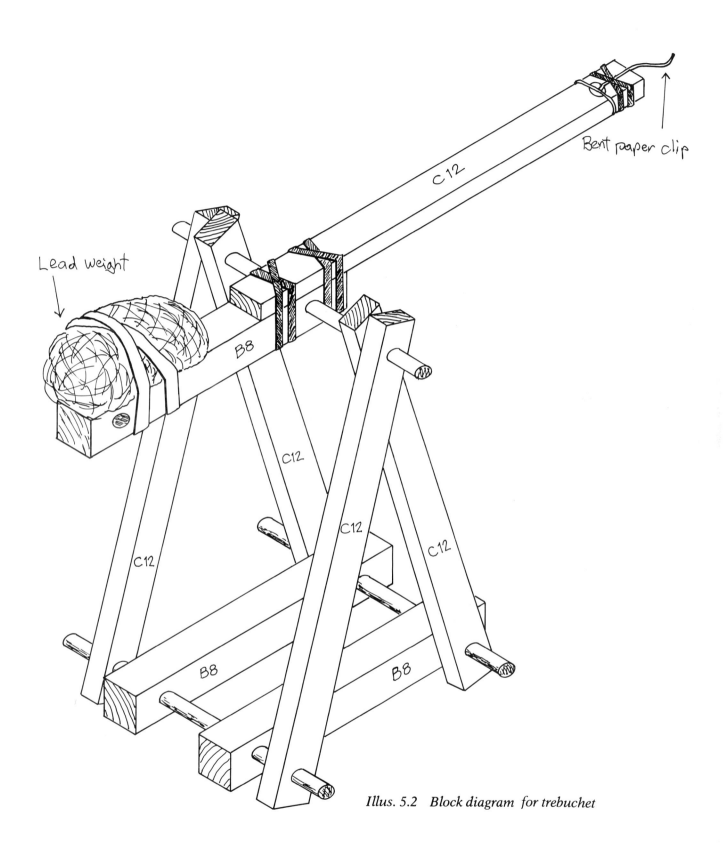

Lead weight

Bent paper clip

C 12

B8

C12

C12

C12

C12

B8

B8

Illus. 5.2   Block diagram for trebuchet

Illus. 5.3   The finished catapult

Illus. 5.4   Block diagram for catapult

Catapult

Materials
- 1 A8
- 2 B8's
- 2 C10's
- 1 C8
- 3 Dowels
- Rubber bands

Instructions
1. Assemble the catapult according to Illus. 5.4. You can see it works on the same principle as the trebuchet.

Twisted rubber band

B8

C8

B8

C10

A8

Twisted rubber band

2. The more rubber bands you twist up for a spring, the farther it will throw.
3. To aim the catapult, jack the front higher or lower by putting blocks under it.

Ballista

Materials

    2 A8's
    2 A4's
    2 C12's
    1 C8
    4 Dowels
    Rubber bands
    Toothpicks
    Transparent tape

Instructions

1. Build the ballista according to Illus. 5.6.
2. The only problem comes in securing the bottom end of the striking arm. Illus. 5.6 shows a rubber band and a dowel. Two rubber bands threaded through the bottom hole in the striker would probably do better.
3. Make the darts of matchsticks, toothpicks, or other small sticks with fins made of transparent tape. One small strip makes all three fins. It is easiest to make the fins bigger than necessary and then trim them down with scissors.
4. To shoot the ballista, lay one or more darts on the pair of A4's but leave the tail ends hanging over the edge a wee bit. Pull back the striker and let fly. It will smack the end of the darts and shoot them forward. The darts should fire straight and far. If they don't, you may have let the tails stick *too* far out beyond the edge of the firing block.

Illus. 5.5   The finished ballista

Illus. 5.6   Block diagram for ballista

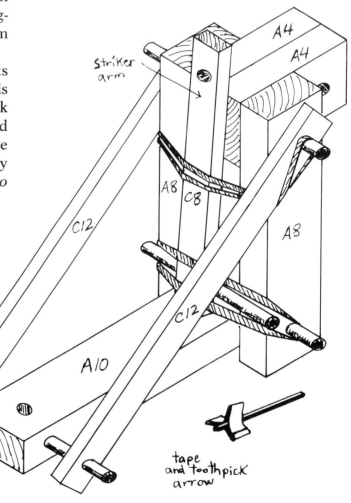

Missile Launcher

The business of attacking castles led from catapults to cannons and finally to rockets and missiles. The missile launcher shown here can shoot a paper airplane swift and true for an astounding distance.

Materials
- 2 A12's
- 1 C12
- 3 Dowels

Instructions
1. Assemble according to Illus. 5.8.
2. Several tough rubber bands are necessary for holding the trigger dowel onto the end of the block.
3. The main launching rubber band can be a single big one looped around the front dowel as shown in Illus. 5.8, or a chain of smaller ones. If the rubber band is too powerful, it will crumple the paper missile or flip it off the launcher.
4. Line up the paper plane in the track of the launcher with the broad end against the vertical dowel trigger. Launch by pulling the dowel back so that the big launching rubber band slides off and shoots the plane.

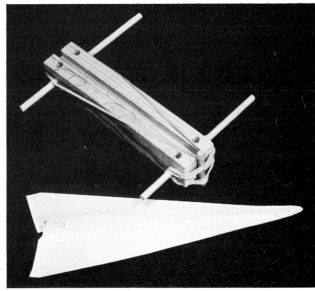

Illus. 5.7   Finished missile launcher with paper airplane

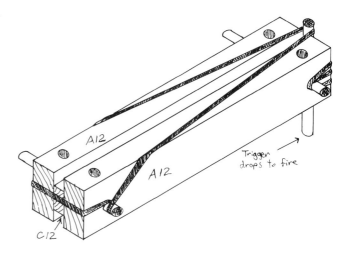

Illus. 5.8   Block diagram for missile launcher

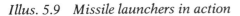

Illus. 5.9   Missile launchers in action

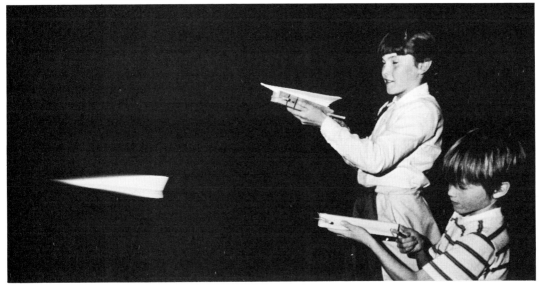

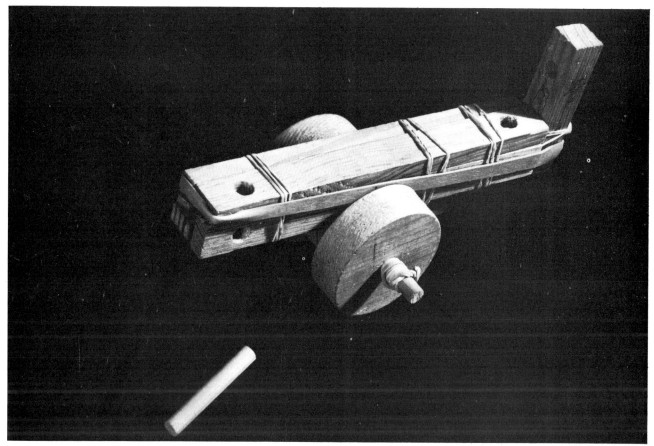
Illus. 5.10 Finished cannon with dowel projectile

Cannon

The Middle Ages and the whole idea of knights and chivalry came to an end when cannons became powerful enough to knock holes in castles.

By about 1350, fairly large cannon served in sieges. They had less power than the latest-model catapults and trebuchets of the time, but they made a frightening, morale-sapping noise, and could hit a wall over and over again in the same spot. It took about a hundred years, however, before the world realized the full extent of what cannon could really do. In 1453, the Turks, using cannons that fired a 500-pound ball, broke the walls of the great city of Constantinople, conquered it, and renamed it Istanbul. After that, no one had any doubt.

Unlike catapults, cannon could also fit into ships or be dragged around on a battlefield. They could fire rocks, grapeshot, pieces of chain, and other things that did a great deal of damage to charging horses and men.

Because of cannon, high walls went out of fashion. Newer forts had low walls of tremendous thickness that could withstand bombardments and support the weight of their own cannon on top to fire back. Because of cannon, heavily armored knights on great lumbering chargers disappeared from the battlefield. In their place came unarmored lancers, hussars, and dragoons on light, fast horses that could overrun a battery of cannon before the gunners had time to reload.

The block cannon here does not in fact work as well as a good block catapult. Nevertheless, it looks something like a cannon and will shoot a piece of dowel well enough to break up a charge of toy soldiers.

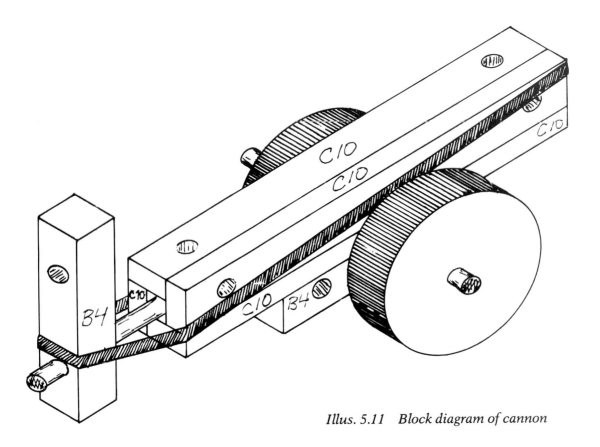

Illus. 5.11   Block diagram of cannon

Materials

    2 B4's
    4 C10's
    2 Wheels
    2 Dowels
    1 Large, thick rubber band
      Small rubber bands

Instructions

1. Assemble according to Illus. 5.11 which shows what size blocks to use. Illus. 5.10 shows where the rubber bands go.
2. The small B4 underneath that holds the axle for the wheels is secured to the barrel by rubber bands that go all the way around it and the barrel.
3. The firing plunger is a dowel that reaches about halfway up the barrel. Use a small rubber band to lash it to a vertical B4 block as shown in Illus. 5.12.
4. Two rubber bands twisted around the outsides of the dowel axle keep the wheels on.
5. Load the cannon by dropping a piece of shot or dowel down the barrel. Fire by pulling back the plunger and letting fly.

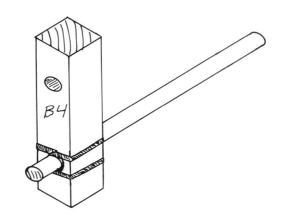

Illus. 5.12   Firing plunger

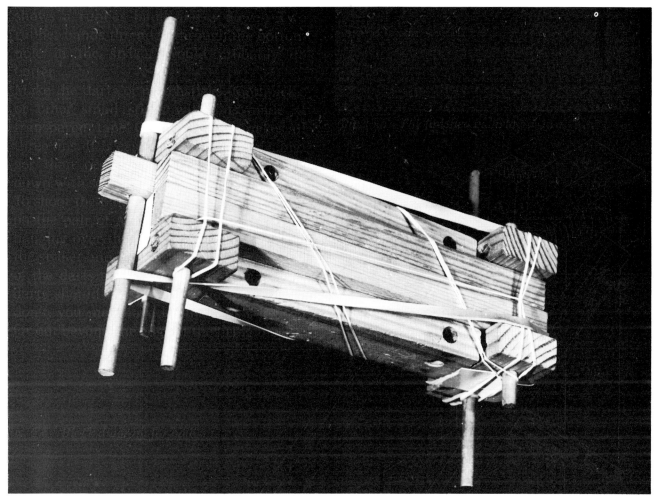

Illus. 5.13   Finished repeating marble shooter

Repeating Marble Shooter

For centuries after their invention, guns had several big problems. A rifleman facing a cavalry charge, or hunting deer, seldom got more than one shot. To reload after every shot meant standing up, pouring powder down the barrel, ramming a piece of cloth down on top of that, then a bullet down on top of that, and yet another piece of wadding to keep the bullet in until fired. Not until the American Civil War in 1860 did anyone figure out how to load a rifle from the back end (the breech) so that it could be done while lying down. Repeating guns that fired several shots at a clip were not invented until the end of the 19th century.

This repeating marble shooter works something like an automatic rifle. When the plunger is pulled back, a marble drops down from a magazine above the barrel into the firing chamber. In real automatic weapons, the recoil of the shot itself does the work of ejecting the spent cartridge, bringing up the new one and cocking the hammer.

This block version is a little clumsy, but it does work. The real problem is finding a place to fire it. Shooting marbles indoors is a bit rude. Outdoors, pavement chips them very quickly, or they get lost easily in grass.

Materials
    2 A8's
    4 A4's
    4 B12's
    1 B8
    5 Dowels
       Poster board
       Marbles
       Rubber bands

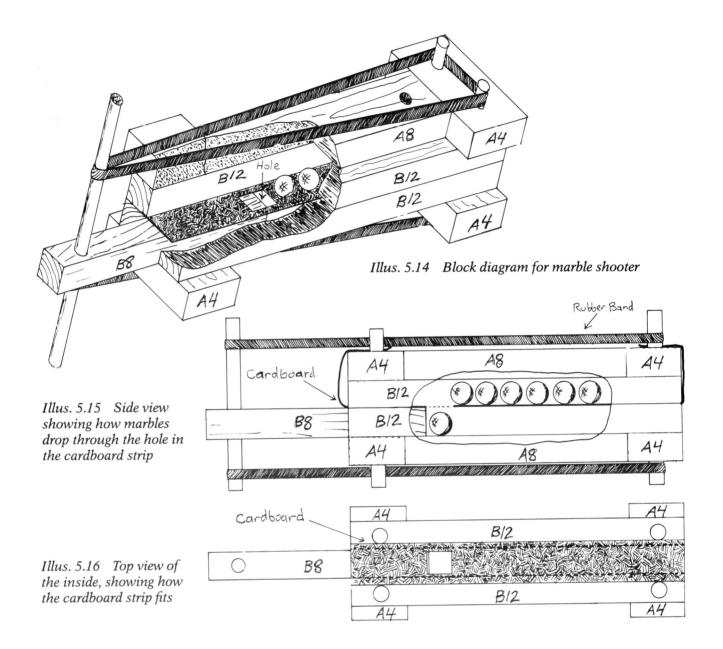

Illus. 5.14   Block diagram for marble shooter

Illus. 5.15   Side view showing how marbles drop through the hole in the cardboard strip

Illus. 5.16   Top view of the inside, showing how the cardboard strip fits

Instructions

1. Assemble according to Illus. 5.14, 5.15 and 5.16.
2. The trick to it all is the cardboard strip that separates the magazine from the barrel. Thin poster board or the kind of cardboard that comes in a new shirt package is ideal. It must fit exactly between the dowels as shown in Illus. 5.16. If the hole is too far back, the plunger won't clear it. If it is too far forward, the plunger won't have enough firing power. The cardboard strip is turned up at the ends and caught under rubber bands to cover the ends of the magazine, as seen in Illus. 5.15.

3. The A8's that cover both the barrel and the magazine are held on only by rubber bands (Illus. 5.13).
4. In Illus. 5.14 the main rubber bands that snap the plunger are heavy "book rubbers" split down the middle. Any stationery supplier will have them. A number of thinner rubber bands will also work.
5. Open the magazine for loading by slipping the turned-up end of the poster-board strip from under its rubber band.
6. To fire, pull back the plunger until you hear a marble drop into the chamber (if you pull back too far, several will drop). Then, aim and fire.

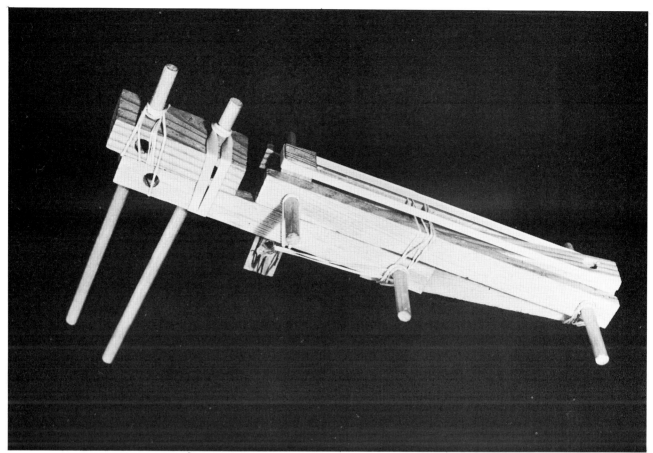

Illus. 5.17   Finished rubber-band pistol with Grip 1

Rubber-Band Pistol

The block rubber-band pistol is not styled after any historical gun. It just shoots rubber bands! The two drawings show two different styles of grip. Most kids prefer the one that has the two dowels sticking down (Grip 1, Illus. 5.17 and 5.19), because it has more style, and a small hand can reach the trigger better from the front dowel. However the other design (Illus. 5.20) is stronger.

Materials
Main Gun:
   1 A8
   1 B4
   2 C12's
   2 C10's
   3 Dowels

Grip 1:
   1 A4
   2 Dowels

Grip 2:
   1 B8
   2 C12's
   2 Dowels

Instructions
1. Assemble according to Illus. 5.19 and 5.20.
2. Notice how, in Illus. 5.17, the rubber bands go around the B4 trigger block. A long rubber band through the bottom hole keeps the trigger forward so that the gun will stay cocked and not fire itself off. Another rubber band goes vertically up to the dowels and around in front of the trigger. This not only helps keep the whole gun together, but also keeps the trigger from snapping too far forward when the gun is not loaded.
3. Hook a rubber band around the front of the A8 and the top of the trigger. Pulling the trigger will tilt it forward and fire the rubber band. Illus. 5.18 shows one ready to shoot.

Illus. 5.18 Repeating marble shooter, left, and rubber-band pistol, right

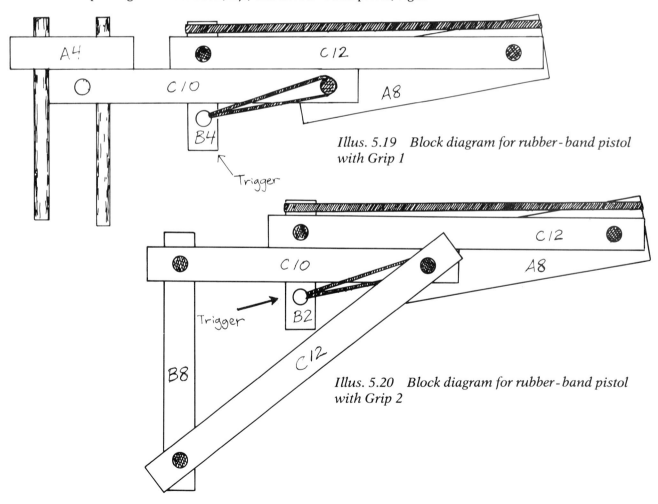

A4

C12

C10

A8

B4

Trigger

Illus. 5.19 Block diagram for rubber-band pistol with Grip 1

C12

C10

A8

Trigger

B2

C12

B8

Illus. 5.20 Block diagram for rubber-band pistol with Grip 2

Parachute Launcher

As a matter of history, the Italian engineer and artist Leonardo da Vinci drew the first picture of a parachute in 1495, but no one actually trusted his life to one until a Frenchman named Sebastien Lenormand parachuted off a tower safely in 1783.

This block project came out of all the shooting contraptions. The idea was to invent a way to fire off a parachute and doll or other payload in such a way that it would stay folded on the way up, then open and come down properly. Such a thing is possible, given a lot of bent paper clips, special folds, and quick-releasing hooks. But besides being complicated, it would require enough rubber-band power to take your thumb off, and no small kid could cock it.

The various kids who worked on the project discovered that by far the best way to launch a parachute is to wind it around a pair of longer A blocks and throw the whole packet underhanded so that the spin keeps the parachute wound up. When the packet starts to fall, the parachute unwinds and looks for all

Illus. 5.21 The parachute launcher being field tested

Illus. 5.22 Parachute and payload

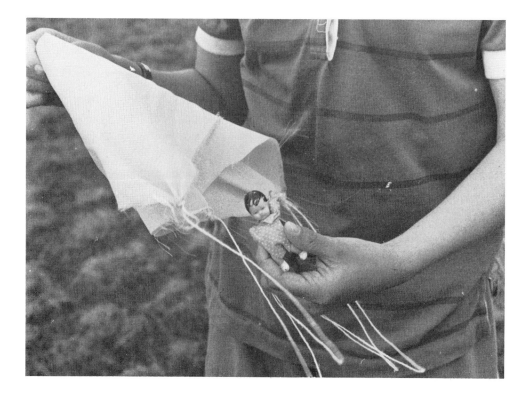

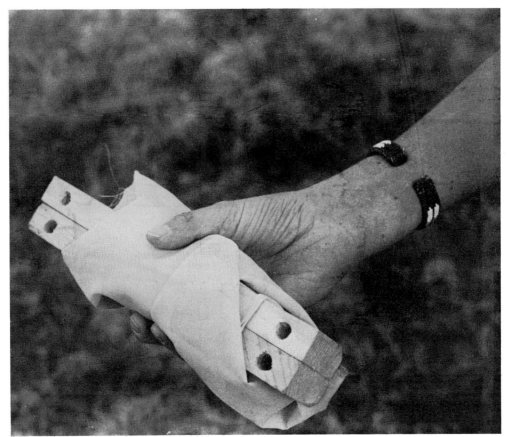

Illus. 5.23   Closeup of wrapped payload package

the world like an astronaut bailing out of a stricken rocket. The only danger is that while you look at the gently descending parachute, the blocks sometimes fall on your head.

Materials

The parachute in Illus. 5.21 and 5.22 was made from a cloth square, 15″ on each side. The shrouds (lines) are also 15″. A **B4** block makes a good parachutist, but dolls can also jump safely.

Instructions

1. Make the parachute using the knot shown in Illus. 5.24 and attach a payload: **B4** block, toy soldier, or little brother.
2. Make launching blocks by simply lashing together a pair of A12's with rubber bands.
3. Lay the payload on the launching blocks and wind the lines and chute around them to make a throwable packet (Illus. 5.23).
4. Holding the packet as shown in Illus. 5.23, toss it underhanded so that as it spins in the air the chute will stay wound on the launching blocks.

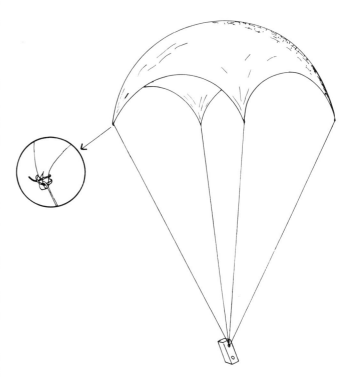

Illus. 5.24   Details of knots and payload configuration

• Index •

· Photo Credits ·

The following have been generous in providing photographs:

Air France, p. 34; Janet Bingham, p. 136; British Tourist Authority, pp. 59, 82, 83, 101, and 104; Egyptian Tourist Agency, p. 84; French Government Tourist Office, pp. 29, 37, and 124; German Information Center, p. 112; Golden Gate Bridge, Highway and Transportation District, pp. 28 and 55 (Robert E. David, photographer); Greek National Tourist Organization, p. 87, p. 89 (Nikos Kontos, photographer); Houston Sports Association, p. 139; Italian Government Tourist Office, p. 40; Japan National Tourist Organization, p. 94; Lake Havasu Area Visitor and Convention Bureau, p. 40; Office du Film de la Province de Quebec, p. 45; The Port Authority of New York and New Jersey, pp. 52 and 53; Sterling Publishing Co., p. 48.